PAUSE, RESET, AND RECHARGE

A Self-Compassion Guide
for Mindful Recovery

by Frances Angeline Rowe

Moving Forward with Gratitude

Love,
Frances

COPYRIGHT

Cover design by: Elizabeth Ward (Positive Energy Publications)
Cover photo courtesy of: Lawrence Shotwell
Namaste photo courtesy of: Allison Carter
Publisher: Positive Energy Publications
PositiveEnergyPublications.com

ISBN: 9798646388927
Independently published in the United States of America

Disclaimer: The content contained within this book is considered 'adult-themed' and is not recommended for young readers. The experiences of the Author are her own and a truthful accounting of her lived experiences was shared. Please note that some of the material may be considered controversial. Therefore, reader discretion is advised. In the event you choose to apply any of the ideas or information in this book for yourself, you agree to accept full responsibility for your actions and resulting outcomes. Individual results may vary.

DEDICATION

Because of your smile, you make life more beautiful.
~Thich Nhat Hanh

Thank you, Mom and Dad. Dad for addiction, nature, nonjudgement, PTSD training and the kindness and love with all of it. Mom, thank you for the unconditional love, the strength, the sacrifices, the grace, the partnership in our work, codependency and compassion training with it all. Thank you, "abuelita"/grandma for the teachings of your values and Spanish language of Panama. Thank you, Irene and Tito for being the best big sister and big brother.

Thank you, Lawrence for your encouragement and partnership. You are my soulmate.

Thank you to all family and friends for the love, kindness and unconditional support. I love you all dearly and am grateful for this in my heart.

Thank you to my clients for sharing your experiences and humility in your personal journey and allowing me to be the gate keeper of some vulnerability and trust.

Thank you Al-Anon® family for support and 12 steps. I appreciate the connection and shared journey of living life one day at a time. Al-Anon® helps me develop a better relationship with my true self.

Thank you to all my yogis and yoga family for allowing me to create my own practice and space to feel safe to come home to no matter if my breath is jumpy, heart heavy, and mind going a mile a minute. My yoga practice has helped me strengthen my internal connection to pause, recognize, allow, investigate and nurture. Now, I'm moving the energy!

Thank you to my many mentors, including Al Greene and Frances Murcherson, and my counselors/therapists through the years, my colleagues (addiction field), and community.

I have so much appreciation to Elizabeth, my amazing writing mentor and editor, who suggested I write my first book!

CONTENTS

A NOTE TO MY READER

During the time I was writing this book, the COVID-19 Pandemic was taking place and had a huge impact on the world. There was without a doubt a huge shift in many lives, including mine. Writing this book was naturally helpful and therapeutic to me in many ways. I had the space and time to do deeper inner work and reflection. I was learning more and more about technology, surrendering to what I had no control over, and focusing on being creative to move forward one day at a time and one breath at a time.

Because of social distancing restrictions, my private practice had to shift all groups into teletherapy. I began using Zoom® with many outpatient treatment groups and continue to do virtual groups. I had no idea when I started this book that the 30 topics would end up becoming convenient teletherapy facilitator topics for me. I shared many of the topics and reflection questions in this book with fellow counselors in similar circumstances, hoping to help.

Having this book in hand (unwittingly) provided me with a format to have a group topic, a relevant heartfelt reading, and reflection questions to allow group members time for personal reflection. This was efficient, flowed smoothly and for me it was a huge stress relief.

I was then better able to focus on the many changes in my life and business, pause and breathe, do my self-care, and become more efficient and balanced as a business owner having more responsibilities than usual. Also, this book was a real-life handbook for me in my personal recovery during this time of extreme uncertainties. To be quite honest, the timing for me to have this material ready at hand as both a 'recovering being' and a 'recovery activist' was a huge help, to say the least. Each topic is unique and specific to the parts of my own personal recovery. From becoming my own healer, fear of uncertainty, asking now what, redemption and finding passion in my losses and grief, these are all topics that will recycle through my own personal recovery when facing my next 'now what?' moment. It's not if, but when, the next 'now what?' moment happens. I am conscious and aware of coming back to my true self and facing the uncertainties with self-compassion and self-love.

The topics in this gentle holistic recovery book are for anyone who wants to pause, reset, recharge, and heal both holistically and mindfully with self-compassion.

This book is great for group facilitators who want to share stories of inner healing and discover relevant topics and questions for discussion. I always say, 'It's an ongoing process' and the beauty of these topics is that you can add new self-reflections and discoveries and grow from all of your experiences. It is a self-inquiry journal for continuum recovery, growth, and healing. For me, I look forward to these uncertainties, and I look towards myself to pause, reset, recharge and recover!

Namaste ~ Frances Angeline Rowe

INTRODUCTION

It is interesting for me to think of what I have control over and what I don't have control over in life. Well, I know that I don't have control over the circumstances we are born into such as life, biology, family, etc. I know that what I do have control over are my choices. Although at times my choices can get complicated as I see various psychological and social influences that in the past had an influence on my choices.

Looking back into my life, I can see the very unique fabric, patterns, threads, and accents that are interwoven into the quilt of my life and existence. In life, I never knew what the bigger picture, the whole quilt, would or could even look like once all carefully sewn together with love like a masterpiece of art. I am an artist at heart and am honored to share with you my fabric and pass on the gifts of beauty of the making of my sacred quilt.

There are so many pieces, messy parts, and some confusing moments while hanging in there and sticking with the making of my own personal life quilt. Thank you for taking the time to go through this journey with me as it has been through the sharing of my pain that has helped me heal parts of my heart that addiction can so easily seep back into for temporary relief. My recovery work personally and professionally has brought much insight and greater awareness. As long as I live, I will be a proud friend, family member, neighbor, colleague, coworker, etc. to those overcoming addiction of any form. It is my passion in life.

So, it is with that thought that I suggest you use this mindful recovery guide in these ways...

1. if you are facing a 'Now what?' moment,
2. if you are a counselor in the addictions field and need a relevant topic to lead your group, or
3. if you are simply someone in recovery and need a gentle and compassionate voice to walk beside you during painful or uncertain moments

This book can be read from cover to cover to support your own recovery efforts, to build upon your own personal recovery plan or you can simply open the book to any page to gently remind you that you are not alone on your recovery journey.

Throughout this book I share many of the practices/tools/programs/teachings that I have learned over the years to help you in your recovery. I have included a Reference section at the back of the book if you would like more information on any of the programs or practices mentioned.

Since many addictions are rooted in childhood experiences, I will next share my own story. The story I will share is a personal story of how and what led me to the path of my own recovery...these topics are connected universally to loss, grief, love, and the pivotal times in my life.

I want you to know that above all else...your recovery path is not linear; life brings so many uncertainties and impermanence. Life brings a constant reminder of what I don't have control over and these topics help bring me back to the now and what I do have control over. For me this allows me to come back to my true self and my values no matter what happens.

MY STORY

My father was a Vietnam veteran and had a military career for over 22 years. He grew up on a blueberry farm in a little town called Burgaw, NC in Pender County. He was a kind, honest, and a big-hearted person. I have lots of respect for my father and his journey through the ups and downs with life. He was a very giving person who really wasn't so attached to material objects.

My grandfather had built a very large tin blueberry packing shed that is bigger than most homes. My father lived like he was on the set of the *M.A.S.H.* show. He even at times preferred to sleep in his cot from his days in the military. He loved to cook and had an outdoor kitchen. He was a man of nature. His happy place was being smack in the middle of the country. He loved his garden. He loved the wildlife and would feed them regularly. He loved fishing. He loved reading in the solitude of the sounds of nature.

My father would look at me with such love and kindness. He always would remind me that I'm so naturally beautiful, smart and wise beyond my years. My father was always a very humble man who asked for nothing. He was a simple country man. I remember he loved his Pal Mal unfiltered cigarettes, cold beer, and being away from lots of people, traffic and loud noise.

My mother is a native from Panama. She was born in the Veraguas Providence along the Pacific Ocean in Panama. She grew up in Panama City. My mother is half Spanish and half Chinese. She has a unique way about her as she is elegant, intelligent, and very loving to her loved ones. My parents met in Panama while my father was stationed there for some years, and my mother was employed with the Presidential Palace as a stenographer. My brother and my sister were already born and in the early years of their life were accustomed to the Panamanian culture and language.

Growing up, I always remember my mother working to ensure I had a good pair of shoes, food on the table, and a home that was safe, comfortable and stable to raise a family. My mother made a lot of sacrifices, sometimes coming home from one job to then get ready for her next job. I remember many evenings when my mom was home resting on the couch watching CNN. I could tell she was exhausted, but she never once complained. She did this year after year. Quite honestly, I felt rich in the sense of abundant love, care, family and sense of connection growing up all together. I will value this immensely forever. I have no doubt that my work ethic is rooted in my mother's role modeling.

My mother moved from Panama to North Carolina some time before I was born, right before my father retired. My father was retiring from an army military career of 22 years and had recently lost his brother, his mother and would soon lose his father who was aging and ill. The blueberry farm he was raised on was quickly changing and no longer what it was growing up. My father loved where he was from and honored his heritage. The impermanence of people, life, health, relationships, the moments and much more I believe all came like a tidal wave for my father.

After my father retired from the military, my parents grew further apart. We moved from Fort Bragg to Burgaw, NC. I was a baby. My mother noticed my father's behavior change and his drinking was all new to her as they met while he was in remission from his addiction to alcohol. I was told he abstained from alcohol for years while dating and courting my mother.

They separated when I was about 4 years old. I know my parents deeply loved each other even though they divorced. As I have seen through ups and downs, how they still showed up for each other in the thick. I remember my mother working most of my life with some heavy hours to be sure we had what we needed. My grandmother from Panama who I call "mi abuelita" moved from Panama to help my mother raise us kids. My brother and sister were 9 and 10 years older than me so they were like my parents as well. My mother traveled often and so having "mi abuelita" and siblings around was comforting.

So, at age 4-5, I was getting more acquainted with my grandmother "mi abuelita" as she now moved into the role of my caregiver. I was learning Spanish and didn't even know what a gift I was receiving until much later in life. She was a stoic lady. She showed very little emotions and was a no-nonsense kind of lady. She was 'old school' in the sense that you respect, listen and do as you're told. She had an energy that was stable, strong, calm and pure. She embodied equanimity to the fullest. I always, even still to this day, admire her energy and her teachings of values like kindness, nonjudgement, non-attachment, love, family, self-care, and spirituality. She taught me Spanish and the beautiful Panamanian culture that has always been a part of me since my childhood, even growing up in the United States.

My grandmother was my protector and I felt secure always with her. We laughed, watched her favorite shows, ate good home cooked meals made with love, and she shared her values of respect, kindness, giving, and family. My grandmother was my best friend. She was funny and encouraged me to be creative, always. She would often say to me, "If you love art, then do it." While she maintained the home, I would get lost for hours drawing, singing, playing or whatever felt fun to do in that moment. My grandmother disciplined me when needed and showed me unconditional love. I learned to respect and appreciate the value of my elders. I have no doubt these teachings helped me build my social skills growing up as I loved the golden rule, "Treat others as you wish to be treated."

It wasn't until I was an adult that I started healing my past. I vaguely remembered an altercation my parents had when I was either 3 or 4. My father had come home intoxicated and my mother was livid. My father brushed it off and I remember my mom throwing something at my father. I'm not sure what happened as I remember hearing a chair fall or something. I just remember feeling panic and running to the other side of the house hoping things would calm down and quick. The energy was intense, and I had no idea how to even wrap my young brain around this. I believe I ran and hid behind another chair to shield myself from the chaos in that abrupt moment.

It wasn't until around age 27 that these memories resurfaced as I hadn't even thought about them in years. They came up when I was in a counseling session with a hypnotherapist who specialized in emotional freedom techniques. During the process, it felt as if I had become lucid in my mind and in a relaxed trance, I shared this story with her as if it was happening right then. I was crying, tensing my body, and my heart was racing. The time went by so fast and 1.5 hours later she brought me back to my conscious presence of time reminding me that I'm safe and I'm here now. I remember that I felt less heavy in my heart as I believe this healing experience allowed me to move the trapped energy that had been festering in my tissues for decades.

This was all new for me and I knew then how deeply I wanted to heal from the pain in my heart. I wound up in most counseling sessions from having tough times in my relationships and feeling the heaviness in my heart. It was those tough times in my life that humbled me to ask for help. Thankfully, I had some amazing counselors guide me to heal. Through counseling, I was beginning to recognize when I would revert back to my painful stories that felt so familiar because of the matching feelings that I was experiencing in my life at the time. It gets complicated at times. Although with patience, time, compassion, and support it becomes less complicated and makes more and more sense.

Pablo Picasso said "Every child is an artist. The problem is how to remain an artist once he grows up." This book is a reminder to grow from our experiences, learn from others and all experiences, and make sure to get to know more of who I truly am and what means the most to me (my values). This is a journey not a destination. It is the process of allowing the energy to move fluidly through this journey and to not get hung up. It is the balance of the work and the play.

Shall we take a walk into this journey of transformation? I'm ready.

#1
FEAR OF UNCERTAINTY

Embrace uncertainty. Some of the most beautiful
chapters in our lives won't have a title until much later.
~Bob Goff

Uncertainty is not knowing what will happen next. It's a sense of powerlessness that can for some bring fear and even control, especially those of us who have experienced trauma. Uncertainty can bring a sense of not feeling safe. This can lead to patterns/habits to protect oneself when facing fears. Many addictions can be rooted from the fears stemmed from uncertainty. It is through conscious awareness of these patterns/habits that I can heal the root of my pain.

Growing up with uncertainty, I had no idea that this would inspire me to write a book. It has been through moments of uncertainties that I gained some of my greatest strengths to serve myself and to serve others who hope for more mental health resiliency. As a child, uncertainty of my father's mental health, my mother's well-being, family finances, shifts in home environments, new caregiver experiences, new language and culture, my parent's separation, and divorce, etc. all were happening simultaneously. It became the new normal. My body plugged into the transitions to survive. I had no control as this became my destiny and my story.

Through the years I have noticed that when I am faced with uncertainty, a lot of fears can be expressed through my body as it goes into fight or flight mode and tries to control. This sometimes looks like neck tension, headache, back ache, sadness or depressive feelings and sometimes even panic. It has been a conditioned pattern that I'm dismantling through awareness and compassion. Looking back as a child, these patterns of reacting and responding helped me adjust and acclimate to an evolving lifestyle so I could survive.

Around age 4 or 5, I remember lots of confusion and uncertainty with my parent's relationship. I felt somewhat of an observer wishing I could help but feeling quite helpless. My father's drinking had spun out of control again after a lengthy period of abstaining before I was born. When that happened, my parent's split and my mother became the emotional, financial, and full-time parent from then on. She made lots of sacrifices to ensure my brother, sister, grandmother and myself had our basic needs met.

She entered Al-Anon® support and found her true self back again. She gained her strength and recovered from the codependency and powerlessness that addiction brings into the family system. My mother was empowering herself to balance all her responsibilities that lie ahead as a single mother with three children and parent from another country. She became resilient and inspired me to be more of who I am through her graceful example.

The fear of uncertainty began at a young age and I really didn't know how to process any of these feelings. I didn't know what to make of it all as I was absorbing the energy of others and my surroundings like a sponge. I wasn't sure if my mother's work would keep her away from me, if my father's mental health would progress, and how learning a new culture and language with a new caregiver "mi abuelita" would all look and feel like.

> *If uncertainty is unacceptable to you, it turns into fear. If it is perfectly acceptable, it turns into increased aliveness, alertness, and creativity.*
> *~Eckhart Tolle*

When facing fear and uncertainty with a compassionate heart, I was able to begin my recovery path. I started to find more peace and acceptance to what happened. Even though many childhood uncertainties had happened, my adult mind attached the story of losses and grief in present moments in the now. I felt helpless and would fear the unknown and the uncertainty, especially if it involved my heart. This pattern I began to realize was not serving me. It was merely separating me from my true self. My mission is to recover and with that said I humbly check in daily looking at what I can do for myself that truly serves me to heal. I get to make choices every day. It's an inside job that is worth the time. It's an investment in myself. There is nothing I can buy to help me or substances that I can take, long-term, to repair the issues that are in my tissues from my childhood. It's energy that must come out to detoxify my soul. I can with loving care allow this process one day at a time to shift and surrender.

Some of the things that have helped me deal with fears of uncertainty are to take even better care of myself, trusting that sometimes in my sleep I can come up with solutions, nurture myself through feeding myself with a warm, balanced meal, spending time around those who show and share love, trusting my higher power and not attaching to a certain outcome but be more fluid and open to other possibilities and doors and spending time in nature.

> I try to view my life circumstances now through the lens of progress versus perfection.

I spend less time focusing on how I can control others and keeping things looking good even in chaos. Now I embrace what happened, look forward to the uncertainty with more trust. It's a reminder every day that some days will be harder and tougher than others, but what can I look forward to, to nurture myself. This becomes more of a spiritual practice reminding me that showing up for myself is my medicine. I look forward to my self-care in the midst of moments of uncertainty. I pause and take a cleansing breath allowing the stale energy that has been trapped in my tissues since my childhood to release with the safety of having my own back and my own heart no matter what. It's an inward place I can go to when in meditation.

> Fear, uncertainty and discomfort are your compasses toward growth.
> ~Unknown

Reflection Questions:
What are some fears of uncertainty that you have faced and overcome?

In what ways have you become more resilient in the face of uncertainty?

What are some growing experiences that you have experienced from facing uncertainty and fears?

What current uncertainty are you faced with in your life?

Where in your body do you sense the emotions that come from the fears of uncertainty? (For example: in your chest, throat, lower back)

What has happened in the past when resisting fears and uncertainties? Any patterns? Has it been serving or not serving you?

What are some things that you currently do to deal with fears of uncertainty?

How can you transform your fears of uncertainty into a connection with something greater than yourself?

In what ways would you like to allow change in your life to help transform your pain/suffering into your strengths?

How can I show up for myself with my heart and my back when facing uncertainty? (Remember no judgement and lots of self-compassion 🙏💗)

What are some of your favorite quotes, mantras, and or phrases about fear and uncertainty?

#2

FACING MOMENTS OF POWERLESSNESS

Don't get upset with people or situations,
both are powerless, without your reaction.
~Buddhist teaching

Powerlessness is fundamentally, at its core, a sense of having no control. Many compulsions and obsessions can develop unconsciously to facilitate the numbing or temporary relief from the discomfort and pain. Codependency is a habit that can be developed when having an overwhelming sense of wanting to fix people, places and things even if this means putting aside your own wellness. Addiction affects all family involved as it's a system that does what it can to survive. This is where the insanity begins.

By the age of 5, my mother and father had divorced. My mother would take me to visit my father who was drinking daily. I remember being apprehensive because I didn't like it when I saw him drinking. I definitely didn't care for his chain smoking either. I would try to put out his cigarettes when he flicked them on the ground walking around. My young mind worried that something would catch on fire if I didn't stomp them out. There were periods where I was in disbelief and shock of how many beer cans had accumulated in a pile. My father would let me know that he was saving them so the gentleman who picked up tin cans would collect them all at one time and pay him for them.

My father seemed like there was not a worry in sight, but by the age of 12, I was festering this concern. It seemed insane to me to be so relaxed with such a lifestyle. My father ate most of his meals cold and always asked for me to just set aside his plate if we brought some food. He drank and smoked instead.

There were some days my father shaved, some days my father bathed, and there were some days I could tell he just didn't give a sh*t anymore. During this entire time, I witnessed my father help others, he gave some of his land to some preacher (who took advantage of my father's active impairment), and he never once asked for any help. He had pride and would rather serve/help others than to take.

I remember feeling the powerlessness in me and it was growing. As much as I wanted to help my father stop drinking, he never asked for my help. As much as I asked him to quit, he would smile, brush me off and laugh. In my gut, I had a feeling that this was going to get harder to witness.

Having no control and feeling powerless over another person you care about, knowing they are harming themselves can bring overwhelming pain and it feels like you can't do anything about it. You can't make them stop and their choices still affect the people that they care about most. It feels so unfair.

Now in my life, I try to focus on what I do have power over versus what I don't have power over. I take my power back by choosing to take care of myself first and looking for the open doors. I also have learned to take things less personally. In the past, I used to wonder why my father wouldn't do what I asked him to do. It made me feel not loved and not important enough.

Now I know that his active addiction had nothing to do with how he felt about me. I saw my father struggling and not even feeling his own feelings. And instead of me interpreting that as his lack of love for me, I recognize now that my self-worth has nothing to do with his story or his detachment from his own feelings.

> *If your compassion does not include yourself, it is incomplete.*
> *~Buddha*

It is through feeling the pain and suffering and the awareness of my feelings with my experiences that I have awakened to know the difference. Then I look towards myself for the love and compassion that I always wanted to get from my father.

> *Love and compassion are necessities, no luxuries. Without them humanity cannot survive.*
> ~Dalai Lama

Reflection Questions:

What are some examples of when you have faced powerlessness?

How does your body respond and or react to your experiences of powerlessness?

Are there any patterns in your powerlessness that create stories that are bringing pain?

What are some of the times that you remember having no control and it causing pain?

What have you learned about yourself when recovering from facing your powerlessness and no control over events or people, etc?

What strengths have you developed from those breakdowns/awakenings?

When facing difficult times experiencing powerlessness, what are some things to help ground and connect with yourself?

#3

CO-DEPENDENT RELATIONSHIPS

The deepest pain I ever felt was denying my own feelings
to make everyone else comfortable.
~Nicole Lyons

Melody Beattie says, "A codependent person is one who has let another person's behavior affect him or her and who is obsessed with controlling that person's behavior."

As a child, I'm glad that some things I remember and some things I have either forgotten or don't remember. Although, through experiential therapy and some deep reflection, some memories have resurfaced. I know that sometimes excavating the repressed memories can help me observe patterns in my thinking that no longer serve me. I am learning that the story has already happened. My mind can either replay, repress, or move the energy

27

of the story into light and strength. I can develop a new story of my growth, strengths, gratitude, survival and forgiveness. It's definitely a process that can be easier than others some days and some days just plain messy.

> *The most painful thing is losing yourself in the process of loving someone too much and forgetting that you are special too.*
> *~Ernest Hemingway*

Recovery work isn't a linear process as it's always ongoing. It has various obstacles and times when finding alternatives to programmed ways of thinking is key in order to keep moving forward.

I know my parents' divorce had nothing to do with me, but as a kid it's so easy to naturally bear the blame, feel somewhat responsible, and feel shame, and guilt. It's hard to explain this natural process in the brain of a developmental 4-year-old. At that age it was so natural to regress into that state where I was the center of everything that was happening to me, somehow I felt like no one else was experiencing this, I was so special and unique to experience these thoughts and feelings. At the same time, I was becoming more sensitive and empathetic to the energies of those around me. In some ways, I would lose myself in the energy of those I cared for and would sometimes even forget how I felt and what I needed.

My mother, I know, struggled quite a bit with the choice to leave my father. I remember vaguely walking the dirt roads with her at the farm. I could feel her fear, sadness, confusion and despair. My mother had no control over a lot of circumstances in her life like my father's relationship to alcohol and how progressive this addiction could become. She couldn't fix this and was far away from the support of her family, culture, native home, and was quite isolated in this small town. I realized looking back, that I was taking on my mother's feelings as my own, not realizing I was developing a co-dependent relationship with her.

A co-dependent relationship often times feels like you are helping those that you love and care for but ultimately you end up sacrificing your own identity which can lead to a detachment from your true self which is at the root of most addictions.

Reflection Questions:
Are you in any codependent relationships?

How does your body respond to a codependent relationship?

What differences do you notice between codependent relationships and healthy relationships?

How have your experiences in codependent relationships helped you take care of yourself better?

How are you able to transform your feelings of guilt from a codependent relationship into your feelings of self-worth and self-compassion?

#4

HEALING SHAME AND GUILT

Grace means that all your mistakes now serve a
purpose instead of serving shame.
~Unknown

Carl Jung says that "Shame is a soul eating emotion."
Shame and guilt are common feelings that people may
experience when dealing with hardships in life, often
they are linked to stigmas around substance use
disorders and mental health issues.

Growing up, I started to build this sense of shame and
guilt. I was not happy with the conditions my father lived
in as I felt it was harsh living. I wanted my father to have
a more conventional home. This was all my opinion
projected onto my father's choices.

In my teens and early adult years, I remember at times
feeling embarrassed or ashamed to bring a friend over or
even share my feelings around this topic regarding my

father. I don't believe I told anyone about my father's drinking and his lifestyle until high school.

Years later while working for a Hospital as a medical case manager, I recollect a female in a meeting asking who my father was. I remember cringing as I know how small towns can be at times. When I replied my father's name, her face looked shocked and she replied, "wow that must of been real hard." She also said this in front of several board members right before a meeting. At that time, I froze and felt a bit naked.

I felt completely unprepared and really didn't know how to reply to this. Quite frankly, I wanted to tell the female in the meeting "what's your problem? Why are you describing my father as a sad disease?" You see, this was not empathy but some sad sympathy card, which felt worse. And further, I was attaching myself to the story, the feelings, and was overwhelmed to even know how to process the stigma and shame that came with it all. I drove home, cried with grief, and took a bath. I thought about why I was so sad. What occurred to me was that I was feeling almost disgraced and judged, like somehow, I was damaged by being the daughter of what she called a 'damaged person.'

> If we can share our story with someone who responds with empathy and understanding, shame can't survive.
> ~Brene' Brown

That same year I was offered a paid internship at an outpatient treatment facility and began my training as a clinician in addiction. What I'm learning about shame and guilt and healing from it may be a lifelong journey. For me, it is an active awareness to detach myself from my painful feelings/story using self-inquiry and love.

> I remember:
> I am not what happened.
> I was a child of a parent who was in their active substance use disorder.

Underlying his choices and relationship with alcohol, there was something way deeper. My father never described what two tours of Vietnam, divorces, losses of family and friends were like for him.

Mental illness, whether it be depression, PTSD/trauma, fears, attachment disorder all are at times overlooked when treating active addiction. The correlation between the two are enormous and makes sense why they can go hand in hand.

In Buddhist philosophy, there is a ''middle path' Approach' to life. There are happy times and there are difficult, tough times. There is cold and there is hot. There is life and there is death. How do I approach life while embracing the philosophy of the 'middle path' ? I accept the tough moments with grace and enjoy the good times as well. There will be both in life. Me hoping that the other side never happens, is creating more pain and suffering. How I perceive these moments takes a bit of compassion and less judgment.

When I judge others like my father, I am actually judging myself. I am feeding myself poison or at least it feels that way. I end up suffering.

Now when I lead groups with recovery of addiction, I feel less charged about sharing the challenge of being an adult child of an alcoholic (ACOA®). In some ways, I am free. I no longer hide behind my shame and guilt that I created in my mind. It was energy that I had no clue what to do with except allow fester in my heart, back, and body. I tucked this away and hoped it would never come out.

Like the lotus flower that grows in the mud, when it blooms it's quite spectacular. This is how I view transforming my guilt and shame. It's messy and quite a bit dirty feeling at times. Although, while embracing the ''middle path' way' and honoring my grief, this growth energy and bloom become this magnificent and extraordinary experience. This feeling is something much greater than the past! It's the beginning of a life changing story with new chapters.

Reflection Questions:
Have you carried any shame and guilt from your past with you?

How has unresolved shame or guilt defined you up until now?

In what ways can you detach from what has happened to you?

What judgments do you have about addiction or those in recovery?

Are there ways that you can transform your pain and suffering into your power or strength?

#5

NOW WHAT? EMBRACING UNCERTAINTY

It is how we embrace the uncertainty in our lives that leads to the great transformations of our souls.
~Brandon A. Trear

'Now what?' I ask myself this question often. It's like a place I come back to over and over again. Life brings lots of moments of uncertainty. That is part of living. It is where I go with my choices that can determine my outcomes.

A 'Now what?' is any form of uncertainty that may trigger fear, discomfort, or pain which can lead to addictive, unhealthy, or high-risk forms of coping.

> *Opening up to uncertainty is what will let you see the door that leads to all your endless possibilities. ~Unknown*

In Yoga, we say it's your practice and it's important to honor the time you take to show up for yourself to pause, connect and do something nurturing for yourself. The 'Now what?' is moving and pausing to receive what we need and let go of what's not serving.

In Al-Anon® / 12 step programs, we ask, 'What do I have control over and what am I powerless over?' I keep the focus on myself and take steps to help recover myself. I learn to have a better relationship with myself. I build support and recognize that I'm not alone in my obstacles and pain. The 'Now what?' in recovery programs is 'Keep coming back...It works if you work it and I'm worth it.'

Whatever you are recovering from, you will face the 'Now what?' It is an active practice of having healthy support from others and oneself, building tools to heal and recover, it's sharing and connection, it's vulnerability, it's nutrition, it's clarity, it's being conscious and aware, and it's ongoing.

Personal reflection and rest can help with moments of uncertainty. It's walking and exercising and moving energy. It's trusting the process and believing that something greater than ourselves exists. It's taking it one day at a time and sometimes one hour at a time. It's accepting that everything is impermanent. It's observing attachments and bringing in more self-compassion. It's being open to the 'middle path' , the good times and not so good times and finding the beauty with them both. It's the balance of all life force energy and opening our hearts to the moments that bring us back to being a student of life.

Reflection Questions:
They say, "when the student is ready, the teacher will appear." How do you relate to this right now?

Do you have any 'Now what's?' in your life?

How would you like to move through your current 'Now what?'

In the past how have your moved through your 'Now what's?'

What patterns have you seen when you were faced with a 'Now what?'

What have you learned from these patterns?

Through active recovery, how can having a good support system and engaging in your recovery help with the 'Now what's?'

What are some opportunities when facing your 'Now what' moments?

What are some helpful habit/rituals that you can practice when facing your 'Now what' moments? (For example, pause, breathe, mentally repeat a mantra like "look forward to _____ and look towards myself", do things that make you feel happy and safe, take a walk outdoors, talk to a trusted friend, do things that ground you to be more present, etc.)

#6

SELF-WORTH AND ILLUSIONS OF SELF-WORTH

You are not your mistakes; they are what you did not who you are.

~Lisa Lieberman-Wang

Self-worth is how I value my true Self. I have experienced self value with my little self (ego) and now more with my true Self. In the past, I didn't know there was a difference. I started to mix the two and started to separate from my true Self, not knowing that was happening. It was easy for me to get so out of balance with this all. I was feeling more valued and self-worth through my academics, my success through work, the income and financial rewards, the exterior appearance, and the physical possessions. It became more and more like an addiction. Once I had a taste of it, I loved how it made me feel. I knew I wanted more of this and I was fixated on the positives that validated the self-worth of my ego.

In 6th grade, I remember the rewards from getting straight A's for the entire year. My teachers gave me lots of praise and such positive feedback. My friends in class asked for my help and the school I was going to placed my class in the gifted program. I enjoyed being able to focus and have less distractions from the various behavioral issues in my prior years. I began to see that if I worked harder and/or made higher marks, I would get more positive attention from my teachers and peers. We even got a teacher once a week take us to a special school to allow us to more fully explore our gifts in various forms through art, reading, hands on projects and creativity. Of course, I loved to do my projects when I could bring in my creative flare. It sure did make learning fun. I was in a public-school setting and had some amazing, impactful teachers in my life. I will always be grateful for the care, help and kindness from my teachers. Teachers are special gifts and I honor their hard work.

In my undergrad at Appalachian State University, I studied K-12 education, teaching English as a second language, and Spanish education. I was saddened to learn that some days I couldn't even go to the restroom if I needed to go, have lunch or a break, and there were many extra out of pocket expenses to travel to two different schools, and to buy student materials to provide for activities. I was really stressed. I would grind my teeth at night and the sound would actually wake me up. I didn't see my quality of life or finances prospering in this field for me. I have gained immense respect for those who make sacrifices to help fellow students succeed. Looking back, it was one of the most mentally and financially challenging jobs I was involved in. For me, the cons outweighed the pros. So, after a while student teaching, I decided to go into a different field.

In my early twenties, I was offered an intern position as a clinician in the addiction field. It was a local private practice that specialized in drug/alcohol assessments and outpatient treatment to help driving while impaired (DWI) offenders to comply with required programs to be able to drive or move forward with legal system. I was designated to be the Spanish speaking clinician in-training and got registered with the State to get certified.

For the first time, I felt the freedom to be creative in my work, grow professionally and learn more, and be rewarded financially the harder I worked. I was paid by client and was given a phone to schedule all those who spoke Spanish only. The Spanish population was growing rapidly, and my services were in high demand. It felt good to be needed and offering a service to help others move forward with their lives to protect their freedom, work and family.

On February 15, 2005, I opened my first business doing drug and alcohol assessments along with education and treatment programs. I provided all my services in English and Spanish. By 2008, my business had hit a record high with scheduled appointments, referrals, full treatment groups, and successful completions so that people could comply with the legal system.

During times of economic crisis, the increase of high-risk choices with alcohol and drugs shot up. I had no idea how much work would be involved. The volume of work had happened so quickly and I was brought up thinking "make hay while the sun shines." I didn't want to take for granted this opportunity, not only to grow as a clinician, but also my savings. I would take a vacation/mental health break every quarter, like paying taxes. I saw a counselor to help me cope with personal stressors. I was easily working seventy to eighty hours a week and it became my norm. My physical tolerance to work was rapidly increasing. In my mind, I was thinking, 'this is the American dream.' In some ways, this was the American dream. The land of opportunity, financial income and prosperity.

It seemed quite natural to be a consumer of my second home, my luxury vehicle, trips, clothes, fancy restaurants, etc. I figured if I'm going to work hard, I might as well play hard. I was grateful to be able to save and start building my retirement in my twenties. It felt empowering as a single person to provide for myself abundantly, financially. It felt powerful. My ego was blowing up in some ways. This was freedom, I thought.

With everything, there is a price to pay. I pampered myself by having a personal trainer, having nice suits, a massage jade bed, and the nicest jacuzzi (hydrotherapy). Even though I had more material possessions and financial freedom, I still felt a void in my heart. I had a heavy heart from some unstable relationships, grief from losses with people I cared for that had passed, and some deep unprocessed emotions from love relationships. I continued to go to counseling but also continued to work more and more. At one point, I was working more than full time and completing my masters in mental health counseling as a full-time student as well. Looking back, I have no idea how I made it through all that work and pressure I put onto myself. My physical tolerance to productivity had hit a record high.

All this stuff, all this business, and all this financial prosperity fed my ego, but I got further from my true self. I was so focused on what had to be done to sustain this lifestyle. I was happy and yet sad. I had fulfilled my dream in my career yet desired to fulfill my dream with more quality time for myself and the people I loved. I am beyond grateful for the opportunities, the gifts from working with others, and the spiritual growth this journey has gifted me. This journey has also showed me the difference between true self-worth and the illusion of self-worth that is dependent on my financial capabilities, productivity, approval from others and material possessions.

> *Work on being in love with the person in the mirror who has been through so much but is still standing. ~Unknown*

True self-worth comes from my self-respect, my care for my balance physically, spiritually and mentally. True self-worth for me is listening to my body and not numbing myself with addictions. True self-worth is allowing my body to detox from all the distractions and to allow my body to be fully present so I can feel, hear, smell, taste and touch in this moment. True self-worth is listening to my intuition and believing I'm worthy of my dreams. True self-worth is devoting weekly time for an artistic date with myself. As I'm am expanding on what true self-worth means to me it includes: nutrition, rest, time to slow down, grieve, be one in nature and time for reflection. It is 'Ahimsa', which is do no harm to self. It is self-compassion. It is saying no more to others. It is doing more of what I love and less of what I think I'm supposed to do to be accepted. It is getting to know myself and asking myself when my heart hurts or feels that void "what do you need?" It is looking towards myself to be the one who gives myself what I always wanted as a little girl but didn't know how. It is allowing myself to create new stories, new possibilities, and new chapters.

Reflection Question:
In what ways have you identified your self-worth?

How would you describe the difference between your ego's self-worth and your true self-worth?

Are there ways you would like to value your true self more?

Have you ever attached yourself to a mistake and mentally lessened and/or physically lessened your sense of self-worth?

In what ways can a lack of self-worth increase your chances to get lost in a trance of unworthiness?

How can a trance of unworthiness feed into your addictions?

What are some ways to strengthen your self-compassion and self-worth to recover?

How can self-compassion help heal the illusions of self-worth?

#7

WHAT ARE YOUR DREAMS?

*Never give up on what you really want to do. The person
with big dreams is more powerful than one with all the
facts.*
~Albert Einstein

What is a dream? It's your thoughts, your ambitions, and your aspirations. A dream is also what comes through your sleep state. The mind's subconscious processing of thoughts all play a role in our dream state. Paying attention to the focus of your thoughts is essential in mastering your dreams fruition. This takes mindfulness and clarity.

> I have had dreams, and I've had nightmares.
> I overcame the nightmares because of my dreams.
> ~Jonas Salk

I remember around the age of seven, I could focus on where I wanted to go or what I wanted to be doing before

I fell asleep. I would awaken the next day first thing in morning to be like "wow it happened in my dream." I felt this was like a superpower. I realized then that the mind is a beautiful, powerful energy.

Many years later, I still spend much of my time visualizing in order to create what I want my life to be like. Reflecting back, I am beyond grateful for what has come true in my life, even the journey through the messiness. It hasn't always been an easy road. In fact, there have been some tears, grief and major shifts in my transformation. I can say that I could not be who I am or where I am without all of it.

> Dream dreams so great they demolish the walls of your cage.
> ~John Mark Green

I guess I could say that many dreams have been born from the hard lessons and opportunities from the unfortunate experiences as well. It is all a lesson. By allowing the energy to move and not get stuck, this can open a new path or other doors, dreams, and larger gains. These experiences can be priceless, from the emotional reward and connection with others and even greater alignment with our spiritual connection.

At age 42, I am focusing more on my balance. I am becoming my own whole-body healer. I'm saying "no" more to others and "yes" more to my needs. I'm healing my emotional state and focusing on my nutrition. I'm making rest a priority. I'm building support. I'm purging more people, places and things that don't serve me well.

I am becoming more of a friend to myself. I am showing up and practicing this more and more and coming back to the pause and connection to my breath.

> Your dream doesn't have an expiration date.
> Take a deep breath and try again.
> ~Unknown

This isn't a linear process, as I will be doing this indefinitely for my continuum of care. It's not if, but when the XXXX happens and things fall apart, that I become my own soldier and resume the position of awareness and self-compassion to look towards myself and connect with my higher power. It is work but knowing that I'm worthy to move through the chaos and have my own back and heart is the ultimate reward.

> Start where you are. Use what you have. Do what you can.
> ~Arthur Ashe

Being an addiction therapist and a yoga teacher has given me the gifts of compassion, forgiveness, patience, the desire for more balance, awareness, and much gratitude. I will forever be filled with this unconditional energy that has been medicine to my soul. Taking time to pause and reflect allows me to move energy and rebalance. As an empath, I need to do this often otherwise I can get out of balance, exhausted and burnt out.

Like today, I was feeling burnt out, so I did this. I go to a very special place in my heart. It is a place I have been going since I was a little girl. It's my father's farm. I will disconnect from technology, recharge and unplug. I will be surrounded by nature and more remote from the exterior world. Nature is greater here and that is good for me. I will be more isolated from a crowd. I will read, walk, listen to the sounds of nature, and I will smell the flowers. My senses will become more alive as I go to a place of less distractions.

I enjoy spending part of my summers in Panama. I go there every year. It is a dream of mine to transition half of my year there as I shift my responsibilities here in the United States. I have a deeper calling to let go of more possessions and appreciate the beauty of simplicity. Consciously dismantling my western mind is a process I use to shift more into my true self and my true desires.

Bottom line is no matter where I am, it is up to me to appreciate what is and connect with where I am. Despite that, I may get burnt out at times. For me, it's a sign to slow down and pause before it gets rough. I have waited too long at times and my body keeps score. I get fatigued, worried, unappreciative, 'stinking thinking' mode, etc. After all, I can become what I think. It is up to me to decide where I want to go and what I make with what I have. A creative mind is usually a relaxed mind. Cheers to more dreams coming true!

Reflection Questions:
What are some of your dreams?

What's consuming your mind?

Are your thoughts aligning with your dreams?

What are some baby steps you can take to get closer to your dreams?

How can embracing obstacles help unleash your deepest dreams?

What will it feel like to accomplish your dreams?

#8

EGO IS NOT YOUR AMIGO – PEOPLE PLEASING

Receive without pride, let go without attachment.

~Marcus Aurelius

People pleasing is a characteristic that some people embody when wanting love and connection, even if it may cause future pain/suffering. Often times it is developed as a way to feel a part of or accepted by others. It can be exhausting and even backfire on the person trying to please others. Sometimes, people pleasing can be dangerous to the self-care of the individual giving and/or helping others. They may feel like a doormat or have feelings of being used. It can lead to poor self-esteem, depression, and increased fears. In people pleasing, we may even see the sides of others that are hurtful and take it personal. As a people pleaser, we may even have a lack of trust in others and it may feel unsafe with our own boundaries.

I was teaching yoga at a treatment facility yesterday evening and this topic was brought up. The topic was people pleasing. In active recovery of perfectionism, workaholism, codependency, obsessive compulsive, and some others, I am dismantling my ego and doing much self inquiry around my small self (ego) and my true self. In the past, I have observed that I have over-scheduled my plate full of tasks, appointments, social events, and even board/committee volunteering experiences. Over a period of time, I became depleted and burnt out. In some cases, it even felt like some relationships would take more and more until I would say "no thank you, maybe next time, I appreciate the invite, or I need to decline to balance all that I have going on in my life." Saying no was essentially saying yes to my self-care, my self-compassion, and my balance.

Reflection through journaling and sharing in anonymous groups has helped me accept and love myself in a non-judgmental way. This process has allowed me to recognize and investigate why I wanted to be at the top of my academics, the top in my work, and just make everything I do look good. At the time, my self-worth was somehow, in my mind, more how others perceived me and what I was doing or wasn't doing. If I did something well, I was worthy. If I failed at something, I was unworthy. This grew into a vicious cycle of much pressure, lack of self-compassion and personal abandonment to my true self. Looking back, I was becoming my worst enemy and didn't even know it.

Starting in 2008, around the economic crash, my business had its busiest year with new clients needing my services. In the mental health and addiction field, it seems to get more hectic, especially during economic crisis or major shifts. Some days I was going in around 8 am and leaving after 8pm. I worked weekends sometimes. I had lots of paperwork. I was on two Boards. I was pushing myself to keep up physically and mentally and I felt exhausted which pushed me further and further away from my creativity. In my mind, I felt so much more worthy because I had a successful business, I was financially and independently secure, and started to accumulate material possessions.

This illusion of staying busy and productive made me think I had made it and became more important. I had more freedom in some ways. Although looking back, I can see I was quickly losing other types of freedom. I was people pleasing more, being more in the past and more in the future hence pulling away from my very present precious moment with my true self, family, and nature. It felt the more I had, the harder I had to work to pay for it all. I knew in my gut that I could do this pace and volume of work for only a certain amount of time in my life. I knew I would have to plan an exit strategy as I felt my body pleading for this. I look back and don't know how I did all that I did. I sometimes still don't know how I do all I do now. This makes me want to do more self-reflection and meditation to lower my tolerance to the insanity of the ego and people pleasing.

What I have learned from people pleasing and the ego is that it isn't sustainable for healing the body, mind and spirit. If anything, similar to a drug, my physical tolerance only increases. Unfortunately, the nature of tolerance tricks me into believing I am handling it all well. Often, this lack of sensitivity and awareness makes me continue to do more and more! It can be progressive. The body will and does keep the score. My body gets tired faster, my nervous system can feel when I am in the fight or flight mode, my amygdala becomes over reactive, my back gets sore, and I feel fatigued.

Through journaling and yoga, I have become more conscious of where my mind goes and continuously repeats certain addictive patterns, and fears. Through this greater awareness, I can lower my tolerance through slowing down, pausing more, and sitting with my thoughts without impairing or numbing them. This work has allowed me to pay attention and notice what I need and desire more. I am still in the process of recovering from people pleasing. This is where my worthiness has led me to honor the now, live more intentionally, doing more of what I want to do rather what I think I am supposed to do. There is much more moderation and balance in my heart and in my life. I am learning to have my heart and my own back more. This is awakening my true nature and my inner light.

Since my yoga teacher training and teaching yoga, I have even more respect for my 5 senses: taste, touch, smell, sight and hearing. I respect the fact that my senses can be my teacher and guide to healing. If I increase my tolerance or change my perception or the state of my senses through addiction, this could trick me and increase my risk to make choices that don't serve me. Then, I can't accurately go by how I feel because my senses are impaired: i.e., 'I can handle more' (so I think). It's really just a form of numbing the senses. This is something for me to consider if it's worth it or not. That is why lowering my tolerance to any mood-altering substances and certain environments can be key to my whole-body healing.

A good practice that I often use is to consciously tune into my body and ask this question: "What do I need?" Then I listen and gift myself what my body is asking me for.

Reflection Questions:
In what areas of my life do I have a high tolerance to_____(e.g.   stress, alcohol, workaholism, people pleasing, perfectionism, toxic relationships)

How has my high tolerance tricked me?

How has your ego served you in the past?

How has your ego not been your amigo?

How has having a higher tolerance to _____ tricked you?

What are you learning about your tolerance and your ego?

#9

BECOMING MY OWN HEALER

Healers are spiritual warriors who have found the courage to defeat the darkness of their souls. Awakening and rising from the depths of their deepest fears, like a Phoenix rising from the ashes. Reborn with a wisdom and strength that creates a light that shines bright enough to help, encourage, and inspire others out of their own darkness.
~Melanie Koulouris

A healer is a person who helps others or self spiritually, mentally and/or physically. Often, a healer facilitates an environment to help heal pain and alleviate suffering. Some healers channel energy from a place greater than themselves to allow a flow of energy to go through the body which helps create more balance in the body. The goal is to facilitate more long-term peace, wellness, and comfort.

> A healer is someone who seeks to be the light that she wishes she had in her darkest moments.
> ~Veronica Tugaleva

Healing for me hasn't always been a linear process. I have had many ups and downs. It's a continuous cycle and my awareness helps me access where I need to move negative or stagnant old energy out of my body.

Yoga, meditation and Pranayama (breathing) has helped me to pause and pay attention to where I am tight, tense, and aching. It is a time to feel all my feelings with self-compassion. This body/mind connection has allowed me then to pay more attention to the root of where the discomfort originates. This is a day to day practice. For example, I notice that my shoulders will automatically tense up when I am carrying a lot of bags into my office. This is an unconscious habit that when I bring into awareness, I can take a breath and allow my shoulders to relax while continuing to carry the bags inside. When I relax and breathe, I smile knowing that I can choose a healthier practice for myself.

In the past, I looked for exterior relief to help with my pain. "What would help me escape, forget and/or numb this feeling?" I guess that's part of my western mind mentality. Sugar, caffeine, alcohol, weed, sex, technology, and so forth and so on can all create short-term relief. If I felt anxious or jumpy, what could I take to calm that? I didn't think about pain/discomfort being energy that needs to move out of my body.

Becoming my own healer is like a frequency where I turn inward to listen to what I need and how I can give this to myself. It's quite liberating to know that no matter what I need and regardless of my circumstances, I can look towards myself and connect with my higher power. It's a process and isn't instant gratification at times. There can be moments of discomfort, awkwardness, and uneasiness. As I lean into this and allow the energy to move through my system, I can connect with my breath to help regulate my mind. The pausing and breathing helps circulate the flow better. I go inward. I am present. I am recognizing, allowing, investigating and nurturing my body, mind, and spirit. I learned this is a form of awareness in my eight-fold yoga class. The term is called R.A.I.N. (recognize, allow, investigate, and nurture).

> To wound others comes so easily, but to be a healer is the rarest of arts.
> ~John Mark Green

Becoming my own healer means I will go into my toolbox and use different tools at different times. Sometimes, my creativity helps move this energy. Music does it too. Nature is a big help. Being connected with those who are uplifting and caring helps. Doing one thing at a time and being present with that moment helps. It's all medicine.

To become one's own healer requires a strong intuitive connection with the true self. It is honoring the body. It requires making ritual time and space to connect with your breath and practice self-compassion. It is feeling all of it and coming back to your own welcoming heart with warmth, love and kindness.

It is creating a home where the void once was, it is no longer numbing that space but nurturing that sacred space instead. It is honoring the special being that is you with all the messiness. It is converting the energy into medicine, one breath at a time.

This is connecting with your higher consciousness and spiritual connection. It is a state of mind that feels "I am safe. I am whole. I am healing." This can be a mantra, a vision and a continuous practice as energy is always moving.

Reflection Questions:
Where in your body do you hold unconscious tension?

What would it feel like if you could consciously loosen up or let go of that tension in your body? (pause now and breathe into the area where you feel the tightness or tension and visualize the tension leaving on the exhale and your body relaxing)

What are some rituals that you can do to calm your mind?(for example, fix a cup of tea, light a candle, burn some sage/Palo Santo to clear the air, take some cleansing breaths, pause and breathe, be in nature, take a break from technology)

What do you want to heal?

How can a personal practice of self-care and intentional breathing help strengthen your healing process?

In what ways can you become your own healer?

When healing yourself, how can you offer healing gifts to others?

#10
ANGER/REBELLION

For every minute you remain angry,
you give up sixty seconds of peace of mind.
~Ralph Waldo Emerson

Anger is a natural, normal, and healthy emotion. It can be a response from pain and suffering. How I respond to anger is important to my well-being. It's energy. It can move out healthy or come out sideways. For example, my anger can come out sideways when I react to a situation versus respond. A mindfulness practice can bring awareness of my attachments, responses, and sufferings associates with anger. 'Ahimsa' in Sanskrit means to do no harm to self and others through actions and speech. This is part of the eight-fold path in Buddhism for healing pain and suffering and attaining enlightenment.

> *When anger rises, think of the consequences.*
> *~Confucious*

Rebellion is responding in the opposite of what may be asked. It can cause waves and even feel as if I am creating a fight against what another may want. Rebelliousness can be liberating and a form of self-expression. It's all in the nature of my choices that can determine my outcomes.

In my teenage years, it was a rite of passage to feel angry and at times be rebellious. It was a period of time that I was questioning the rules, laws, and demands asked of me. It was a period I felt I deserved to blow off steam and to have fun. I was sixteen and had my freedom with my driver's license! The movie *License to Kill* was out and it was part of the culture to associate your driver's license with absolute freedom. Suddenly, I could go to my friend's houses and go see live shows. We could go to the beach and go to parties! Curfews, drinking age, and adult lectures all seemed like a complete drag.

I continued to go to school and make good grades as I knew for me more freedom would come with my education. I waitressed and worked at a local arcade/amusement park and knew I had more to explore in my career settings. I knew having others tell me what to do was temporary and to hang in even though I was, at times, fed up. I did learn that the harder I worked, sometimes I could have higher financial gains and for sure, superior praise.

Anger and intolerance are the enemies of correct understanding.
~Mahatma Gandhi

Music and art really allowed me to express my rebellious feelings more vividly than I could have ever imagined. Nirvana, the band was classic to my ear. I loved the way the music made me feel. The song, *Teen Spirit* was angry, happy, sad, energetic, relaxed, and confusing all in one. It really resonated with me at that time. It was like the beginning of a movement and I felt that I wanted more freedom and self-expression. I felt like I was at a crossroads of finding myself and making my own choices verses listening to others and doing what I'm told.

Being the youngest child and always having grownups around me, it felt quite normal to listen and comply. Being a teenager during the 90's, I had some legendary music which greatly influenced my self-expression. I remember wearing relaxed jeans (Levis® button fly, my favorites), a soft flannel, flip flops, Vans® or Birkenstocks®, and essential oils. I loved my art class in high school, I took it all four years and loved my teacher who retired my senior year. I created some of my favorite pieces during that block of time. I painted a naked woman in Cubism, abstract style. I was stoked that it was in our local mall even if it was provocative. It was a statement and it was free and wild. I love that painting as it was a way to express the beauty and freedom of self exposure and sensuality. That same painting was displayed in our local art museum recently. Art and music always lives! It truly has been my passion as long as I can remember.

Comfort was the style during my high school and college years. I was a flower child at heart. In 1995, I moved to Boone, NC and attended my undergrad studies at Appalachian State University. This place was beautiful and truly a special place still to this day. Waterfalls, Blue Ridge Mountains, organic everything, a super laid-back environment, and lots of great live music. It was a 'dry county' with no liquor, yet tons of weed and brewed beer. It was a bit cold for my warm-blooded nature, but it taught me how to drive in crazy snow and ice conditions, find more of myself individually, and appreciate more my family and home when I returned back to the beach.

During my sophomore year in college, I had quite an awakening. I was underage drinking and was involved in a bad accident. I was a passenger in a golf cart on a local island from my hometown. My friend driving was drinking as well. I was ejected out of the golf cart that was moving over 30 miles an hour. I had a compound fracture to my right arm. This accident changed my life permanently. I had multiple surgeries, months and months of various opiates from the morphine pump to other opiates prescribed from my orthopedic surgeon. I was a walking pharmacy for some time. I was half a millimeter away from having permanent nerve damage to my right arm. And because I'm right-handed as well, that year was a challenging one to say the least.

I have heard that a breakdown is also like an awakening. Well, I like the way awakening sounds. During my recuperation, I felt a bit lost and saddened to see how some of my friendships were no deeper than getting high, having fun or just hanging out at a party. I learned quickly who were my true friends, who was there for support, and that recovering from the withdrawals of heavy opiates and a major traumatic injury is a pain in the XXX. I survived and am stronger from this. I respect pharmacology and know that it is short-term relief. During this time, my heart was recovering too because of some broken relationships, and I hadn't developed the tools to recover. Being numbed by drugs was nice to not feel very real physical pain, but my emotional pain was numb too. I felt this repressed emotion would eventually come out. When in active recovery, I feel that love and support can be some of the best medicine.

Well, my anger and rebellion shifted after this major health setback. I was awakened to the fact that I am not invincible. I was more careful with the dangers of impairment from substances that could happen to anyone, including myself, pretty quickly. I realized that my energy could either be numb or I could move it through my system differently. I was still exploring this concept as this was all new. I was healing from shame as this accident had nothing to do with who I am, even though I beat myself up mentally for making such high-risk choices.

My mental impairment in those moments, prevented me from clear executive thinking, especially in emergency situations. My anger and rebellion all were psychological influences and the people I spent time with were part of my social influences. Both psychological and social influences affected my choices.

At the end of the day, my choices are important to my outcomes. This was a pivotal time in my life as it eventually opened other doors in my path. I spent much time thinking of my grief, losses and was stuck. It was through these moments that I learned that these experiences can truly happen to anyone. It is having a greater awareness of the nature of my choices and being mindful of my social and phycological influences that help me protect what's important to me. Growing pains can be a xxxxx.

Reflection Questions:
What are some examples of psychological and social influences that have affected your choices in the past?

What are some of the negative outcomes that have come from impairment?

What unexpressed anger may be showing up as rebellion in your life?

Have you noticed any patterns of emotions/feelings that create a craving for short-term relief?

What are some positive ways to cope with anger?

How can pride block my heart?

#11

MOVING ENERGY THAT NO LONGER SERVES

Energy flows where intention goes.
~Unknown

Energy is the feelings, vibrations, thoughts, tensions, or forces that can come from interior or exterior places. Energy can bring pain, pleasure, confusion, and clarity, etc. Energy is everywhere like nature, other people, large groups, internally the way I feel, etc. It can flow out of us, through us, or it can get trapped in the body. My body, tissues and nervous system can absorb energy. It is important to allow my body to detox/purge any energy that doesn't serve me. I'm finding ways to even allow past energy to flow out of my system. This is a process and requires self-compassion, self-love and conscious awareness. I love the phrase "good vibes only" and this helps me redirect my energy and be aware of how my thinking can affect my energy.

Yoga and Twelve Step Programs have helped me organically purge and let go of energy that's not mine and accept what is mine.

Yoga is a personal practice that allows me to connect my breath, my structural body, and my mind together. Practicing yoga allows me to inquire where my mind, body and spirit may be out of balance. "One breath at a time" allows me to remember to breathe and pause and move to my next breath. I don't have to have it all figured out. I can trust that I can focus on this moment and move to the breath to care for my body. I love the phrase "take a deep cleansing breath." It reminds me that my breath is life. Each intentional breath nurtures my body and allows me to heal and thrive.

Pranayama are breathing exercises in yoga that can be included in one's daily yoga practice. Research shows that Pranayama in yoga can actually create more lubrication in one's eyes, lower inflammation in the body to heal, reduce stress and create abundant relaxation.

I have four favorite Pranayama exercises that I include in my yoga sequence when teaching:
1. Alternate nostril breathing
2. Inhale/exhale/retention (Puraka/Kechaka/Kumbhaka)
3. Ocean breath (Ujayi)
4. Tonglen breath (come back to your intention and awaken compassion)

I share these breathing practices to help regulate the mind, lower stress, focus more, and feel naturally at peace and happy. It's amazing to know that I can develop my own practice to get the outcomes of what I want and to protect what is important to me. You don't have to buy anything or take anything to master this simple, yet beautiful connection with mind and body. The key is to pause, inhale, pause, exhale, deep cleansing breaths, no judgement, remembering that this is your own practice and it's what you need to heal and be present with you! It truly can be a gift that continues to feed the soul/spirit. When practicing, this is a sustainable and successful way to approach discomfort and unease in the body and mind. Intentional breathing can help move stagnant energy and make more room and flow for energy that is serving to the system.

12 step programs are recovery programs that are held in groups (i.e. AA®, CoDA®, Al-Anon®), but also can be read in a daily devotional individually. There are many kinds of 12 step groups combined with other recovery methods. Traditionally, I enjoy a local Al-Anon® group.

The combination of yoga and 12 steps is a nice adjunct. I teach a Y12SR® yoga designed by Nikki Myers. This style is an adjunct to 12 steps and recovery. It's combining the steps while recognizing that there are "issues/trapped energy that reside in the tissues" and the yoga practice and certain postures allows the movement, pausing with any discomfort, feeling the body, and cleansing the body with intentional breathing.

This is a mindful practice to heal the mind, body and spirit.

Walking is one of my favorite exercises. It's a great way to move the body and breath. I enjoy walking on the beach, lake, park, river, and especially with some sunshine (straight vitamin D). It's great to scan/check in with the body feeling my feet, my toes, my lower back, my neck and shoulders. When walking I consciously connect with my senses. Seeing water, watching a sunrise, leaves swaying on trees, glancing at a dolphin or a rabbit is me being in the moment. Hearing the waves or geese is being present. Smelling flowers, the fresh air is tapping into the present. Tasting a cup of water, a cup of tea is connecting with the body right now. Touching my hands and feet, digging in dirt is grounding. The options and varieties of sense stimulation are limitless. The beauty of using our senses and connecting with our favorites is not only therapeutic but quite inexpensive as most of my choices involve nature. Try it! Observe your well-being grow as you practice more mindfulness and connection with nature. This can be something to look forward to almost like a treat/reward/gift. It's a sure way to enhance dopamine, the pleasure chemical in our brain.

There are many creative ways to move energy that no longer serves, like yoga and 12 steps. Pranayama is an excellent way to activate your parasympathetic nervous system. This allows your mind to calm and be present, one breath at a time. The practice is to be present when the breath becomes jumpy, short, tight, etc. This is also a good time to observe your body posture. Are your shoulders and neck tightening or "crunching" together? If so, pause and inhale through your nose, pause, and exhale. The awareness with practice will show up more and more. Remember, it is your practice and keep coming back.

Reflection Questions:
Do you feel, at times, an immense sensory overload?

Do you have a quiet space at home that can be a place to breathe and meditate?

What does the word "pause" mean to you and how can this practice with your connection to your breath benefit you, especially when you're busy?

Where does your body hold tension and stress?

How do you like spending time outside? Can you create a combination of nature and either a walk, sitting in a comfortable spot and observing nature, and/or connection with a hobby/sport that includes moving energy?

#12

REFRAMING VULNERABILITY INTO STRENGTHS

What makes you vulnerable makes you beautiful.
~Brene' Brown

Vulnerability for some is viewed as weakness, exposure to get hurt, and unsafe. In a therapeutic view, vulnerability can be courageous and a strength. These two meanings are the opposite. Perspective is the context in understanding what this means for me.

The 'middle path' for me with vulnerability is the yin and yang of the situation. Vulnerability can have both some pros and cons. I like to examine the 'middle path' so that I'm not blocking some of the greatest gifts from the connection of my emotional body. This allows me to grow closer to my true Self verses my ego.

For example, for almost two decades, I viewed my sensitivity as a curse. I felt so many feelings from myself and others. If they were great feelings, I was elated. If it was sadness, anger, or negativity, I felt drained, sad and even confused. Some people told me, "You're too sensitive!" I have heard people say, "Frances your problem is that you wear your feelings on your sleeve!" This made me think that something was wrong with me. I had a flaw that would bring me down. I thought back then that I was emotionally weak. With this perspective, I grew quite shameful of myself. I would even get frustrated and angry with myself wondering, "What in the heck is my problem?" I had no idea that I was doing harm emotionally to myself. All I knew was that I was broken and needed to be fixed. What a harsh way to view oneself. I thought it was quite normal to berate myself to toughen up. "No pain, no gain!" I understand now why it's easy to numb the feelings that may come across as a weakness/vulnerability. I avoided the exposure of any judgement from outside myself, yet internally, I continued. Because of this, I developed more control and perfectionism.

Little did I know, I was merely repressing some of my greatest assets/gifts. It is all in perspective. As a child, I have always been an artist at heart. Art to me is fluid. There is no right or wrong. I could start a painting, mess up, and then find a different way to fix or create a painting. It all was a part of the process. It was a creative flow that had many directions. It wasn't rigid. It didn't tell me I'm wrong. I could be all of me and be happy.

Also, I didn't like to waste my art supplies as I knew they would last longer if I took good care of them. With this in mind there were no mistakes, only different routes. As a kid, I knew this in an abstract way. Art has always made sense to my mind.

I applied these concepts and perspective of how art and my life in the real world could be similar. I learned later in my mid-twenties that my 'weakness' could potentially become my biggest strength/gift to help me become my best Self. This was enlightenment for me. It was like the light bulb came on in my body. My experiences, even the difficult ones in my life could open a door that could channel something greater than myself. It felt spiritual. It felt like it was the right thing at that time to share and listen to others who exposed their vulnerability. Like my art, there was a moving energy about this experience. It wasn't stagnant or repressed. A new door/perspective was illuminated. I was gaining momentum and strength with this new perspective. It made me feel alive and thriving.

Another perspective in looking at my sensitivity is the identification that I am an empathetic person. This characteristic helped me relate to others that came into my office for counseling. In my practice, I have many who feel vulnerable and even beat themselves up for making mistakes. I have compassion with most of my clients as I can relate to many of these emotions. Guilt and shame can be toxic energies that can manifest dis-ease to the body, mind, and spirit. It is critical to name it, move it and open our heart. I enjoy helping others reframe their vulnerabilities. I learned that it's so easy to identify ourselves with our problems and essentially create or relive a story that doesn't serve us. It's like a trance that if not conscious and aware could continue to win. I have to constantly remind myself: I am not my mistakes, weaknesses, nor problems. That's not who I am.

Most of my clients are caring, family oriented, responsible, hardworking, and kind people. We ultimately are not our mistakes or problems. Our values and what is important to us can be a greater indicator of our true Self. Taking accountability, forgiving ourselves or others, and learning from our experiences can lead us to other doors. This takes much compassion for others and ourselves. This can be challenging. Inner peace is my focus now. There can be waxing and waning moments as healing through pain/suffering can have many layers. I have heard it's like peeling an onion. Having an active recovery plan and support helps stabilize challenging moments and can bring hope and strength to look at perspectives that help grow, heal and recover. This is an ongoing process.

Like vulnerability, the word surrender has different meanings and perspectives. From a therapeutic perspective, surrender is not a weakness. It can be a strength to not push, fight against, or run, etc.

I used to be scared of the boogie man as a little girl. The more I fed into that fear, the stronger it got. Surrendering to the fear of the boogie man, is like listening to my story and not getting charged negatively by my story. I first observe how I feel when I believe the story I have about the boogie man. How much is true about the boogie man? Is my story all true? At the end of today, what feeling do I want inside? Is it safety, protection, peace, or something else?

Vulnerability and surrender hold new meanings for me, especially during difficult times or when helping others. For me, it's "offering chaos a cup of tea." Surrendering to what is doesn't have to be viewed as a defeat. For me, it is accepting what happened, getting to know all perspectives while developing more compassion for myself and others. It is hard to mentally feel compassionate to a mean person. Although it can be an art to not attach ourselves to the story. Forgiveness isn't always necessarily for the other person. It's often for the healing and freedom for the person stuck in the past to liberate and move forward. I am still working on this and will continue as it's my peace and serenity that is the desired outcome. Being patient, having forgiveness in my heart and becoming my own friend allows me to build perspective.

Reflection Questions:
How do you interpret vulnerability and surrendering?

How can you surrender to the uncertainty?

Have you ever defined yourself from a mistake you made in the past or circumstances that happened in your life? Can you find other doors from your story?

Do you have a story that gets you stuck or brings pain? Are there any patterns?

What is important to you? (Family, freedom, health, spirituality, etc)

Have you developed any passions from any obstacles in your life? (Like an alchemist)

In what ways can developing personal passions lead you to your true Self?

What does 'trusting the Universe' mean to you?

What does 'trusting the process' mean to you?

#13

THE BREATHING CONNECTION WITH THE MIND, BODY, & SPIRIT

Breathing in, I calm my body. Breathing out, I smile.
Dwelling in the present moment, I know this is a
wonderful moment.
~Thich Nhat Hahn

Jack Kornfield says that "Breathing meditation can quiet the mind, open the body, and develop a great power of concentration." Breath is life. There is the parasympathetic nervous system and the sympathetic nervous system. The breath, the mind, and the body all respond and/or react in many situations throughout the day. The nervous system is all connected to our skeleton and structural body like our spine, neck, and tailbone.

Our tissues have memory. My habits and patterns can either help me or harm me.

With PTSD and other historical trauma experiences, the brain can be conditioned to react quickly to survive. Even after twenty years of having some grief/losses, I still have a tendency to react to any perceived threat mentally and/or physically. In the past, I had no idea how my breath could help regulate my mind. I was just plugging in and reacting to feel safe or better. The mind can feel or perceive threats in various ways, especially if it triggers a flashback of an emotion that reminds one of that feeling. The amygdala is the part of the brain that stores emotions like fear, sadness and anger. I have recognized when I have had an overactive amygdala. In this awareness, I can do some self inquiry. I can "recognize, allow, investigate and nurture (R.A.I.N)." The "R.A.I.N" method was a technique I learned in my eight-folded yoga teacher training. It's as if I am sitting with the sensations and feelings verses running and numbing them. The biggest shift for me is when I can identify that my amygdala is being over-reactive. Then, I know the next step is to pause, breathe, and look towards myself to "nurture" and give myself what I need now. This takes immense self-compassion.

In yoga, I have developed some personal mantras that help calm my mind.

"I am safe. I am calm. I am worthy. I am healing. I smile."

Mantras can be a nice tool to help lift up the positivity in the mind and shift negative thoughts to more gratitude.

> "I am healing and developing new rituals to allow my breath to have a voice. I will be clear minded to pay attention to what my body is telling me so I can listen and give myself what I need."

In my western mind, I could see how I would numb, distract or run away from my discomfort. For example, in a social setting I would drink to fit in and relax. After a few drinks, I didn't feel the tension from a long day at work. I didn't feel the worries in a relationship. It was like my pause button to blow off some steam. I have no judgement on this as it can be healthy in moderation. Unfortunately, I was spending less time making choices and building rituals to help me heal the root cause of my tension and frustrations. Ultimately, I was trapping more energy that wasn't serving me verses purging/detoxing and clearing the energy that was not serving me to be my true Self.

How do I "offer chaos a cup of tea?" Some rituals I have developed when facing higher stresses are taking an Epsom salt bath with my favorite essential oils, aromatherapy, walking outside at the beach or in nature, drinking plenty of water to hydrate daily, healthy nutrition, resting to repair my body and mind, allowing my dreams at night to be sacred time to repair stressors, reading, less technology, meditating, having a cup of tea, having a creative date with myself, journaling, going to a 12 step meeting, attending a restorative yoga class, calling a friend/loved one, doing a vision board, watching a movie (I love black and white classics). The beauty in this is you get to customize your own healing, relaxation, and re-connection process/rituals. This is a practice and an ongoing process. It is not linear as it is a work in progress.

The healing vibes that I desire are peace, calmness, creativity, compassion for self and others, abundance, love, joy, and grace. With one breath at a time, I can pause, observe, do some self-inquiry with a whole lot of compassion, allow my feelings, and look towards myself to nurture and move the energy in a positive, healthy way that serves me long-term and allows the root issue to heal.

> *Clearly recognizing what is happening inside us, and regarding what we see with an open, kind and loving heart, is what I call Radical Acceptance. If we are holding back from any part of our experience, if our heart shuts out any part of who we are and what we feel, we are fueling the fears and feelings of separation that sustain the trance of unworthiness. Radical Acceptance directly dismantles the very foundation of this trance.*
> *~Tara Brach*

Reflection Questions:
How do you respond emotionally and physically when you perceive a threat or fear-based emotion?

Do you have any mantras that can help with stressors?

When faced with higher stressors, what are some grounding techniques and/or activities that can help regulate your mind?

How do you "offer chaos a cup of tea?"

Have you seen any patterns in your chaos or perceived threats or fears?

What do you need when faced with discomfort and how can you look towards yourself for safety or comfort? What can you do?

When conditioning your body and mind to a new response, what are some of the rewards and benefits? How would this feel to receive the healing vibes you desire?

#14

THE GIFT OF HELPING OTHERS

The purpose of life is not to be happy. It is to be honourable, to be compassionate, to have it make some difference that you lived and lived well.

~Ralph Waldo Emerson

Service work can be volunteering for a board/committee, helping a neighbor, listening to a friend in need, helping a lost animal find their home, or even having less judgement and more compassion for those who struggle with addiction. It is an act of kindness with no expectation of anything in return. Sometimes it's like sharing our gifts, gratitude, heart, and care to others with lots of generosity. It's great to do service work that inspires you and/or an area that you have a passion. I have made some amazing friendships and developed much connection from serving others and vice versa. There have been so many inspiring people in my life who have helped me grow and heal. I have had some wonderful mentors as well. Service work can remind me of the kindness, the love and goodness in the Universe. It gives me an immense sense of connection as well, which can help heal the heart.

I am amazed by the many moments of pure serendipity that have come about from staying present and offering compassion. I have made some incredible friendships through meeting folks who share interest in work, in therapy, yoga and art. The sharing of our ups and downs in life have brought much connection and compassion.

> *Let's root for others and watch each other grow.* ~Unknown

I love this quote as it's really rewarding to plant a seed or a small plant, water it, nurture it and see it grow and thrive. Cultivating a garden/plant can be therapeutic and grounding. It's a lot of work but it's great to see the transformation. Today, I was speaking with a counselor that I supervised to help through their licensure process. It is a gift to see a counselor grow and move forward with their goals. I remember how my own clinical supervision helped me grow and build my confidence. One of my best mentors would always tell me "honor your grief."

When teaching Y12SR yoga for recovery, it's beautiful as our group shares for 45 minutes about a recovery topic and becomes vulnerable and real and then the next 45 minutes we practice yoga to move the energy and restore our body, mind, and spirit. We all share about our addictions, recovery, and we listen with honor. After someone shares, I love that we say "let's root, ground and take a deep breath with xxxxxxx." We all pause and breathe together. It's a beautiful, safe and sacred gesture. This process allows me to reflect, feel, connect and nurture my heart.

For me, it's a gift to see a person uplifted, given hope, and some compassion in difficult times. In Al-Anon®, I have made many friends. I have had many opportunities to share my story with the group. While sharing my story, I was always a bit worried of what others might say/think or if I even wanted to expose myself that deep. Afterwards, I felt relieved, supported, less heavy in the heart, and it was an energy release. I feel that there is still a tremendous amount of healing for me to do, yet I am patient with self-compassion as this is all a process. I feel safe to share in confidential groups as I know it can bring limitless gifts to my soul. My favorite 12 step meetings are when I can listen to another person's story and it helps encourage me to work on myself and keep the focus back on myself and what I have control over. This process has dismantled the core root of some of my shame and guilt. It is freedom!

I remember around age 11, I had an elderly neighbor. We became friends despite our age difference. I would go visit and chat with her for an hour or so and we would share our creative thoughts. She was so kind as she always gifted me with a cold soda. It was a treat as growing up we didn't have soft drinks or junk food at home, only special occasions. One day, she said she had cleaned out a closet and found a doll making kit. She recommended I take it home and enjoy! She asked for nothing and gave this from her heart. When I got home, I was elated as she encouraged my creativity. I put the doll and kit all together. It was fun. The doll, I remember, had a white dress I made and looked like the picture on the box. The next time I went over to visit my neighbor, as usual she poured me a cold soda. I was so happy to give her the doll. She smiled and gave me a great, big hug. She and I had a special relationship and our connection made me value my neighbors, even still to this day. I am grateful for the kindness and generosity from my neighbors.

All in all, I feel it's through gifting and helping others that the heart can heal. It's doing for others with no expectations. It's karma. It's what goes around comes around. Those who have shared with me their recovery including the messy parts, have given me a gift. It's like keeping the circle positive and going. Others have given me courage to share my messiness and feel safe and supported. My self-compassion has grown leaps and bounds from moments, experiences and the gifting of compassion from others who have courageously shared. It's passing wisdom down to help others suffer less. It's a priceless gift.

Reflection Questions:
Describe a time in your life that you felt your best. Who was there? Where were you?

If you were to give your time or service to others, where and/or to whom would you like to give time, energy, compassion? And why?

How has a mentor, couch, teacher, or friend ever gifted you with compassion, encouragement and support?

What are you grateful for?

#15

RESILIENCE AND SELF-CARE

...If you feel "burnout" setting in, if you feel demoralized and exhausted, it is best, for the sake of everyone, to withdraw and RESTORE yourself.

~Dalai Lama

Self-care is the action of caring for oneself physically, mentally and emotionally. It can include balanced nutrition, adequate rest/sleep, hydration with water, exercise, safe choices and environments, setting healthy boundaries, healthy relationships with self and others, time outside in nature, stretching, time for reflection, building support, spirituality and time for creativity. There are many forms of self-care and the beauty of this action is that it can be customized to your own personal needs. It's through our ups and downs that help awaken us to what's important for self-care.

The key for me is to look towards more balance and moderation in all areas of my life. In Sanskrit, "bramacharya" means moderation and right use of energy. It is a universal morality to help interact with self and others.

When my self-care is out of balance, I become more irritable, depressed, angry, go into my victim mindset, and feel burnt out. The disconnection with my true Self can be re-activated. I can lean more towards my ego. I catch a cold or feel run down. My immune system can suffer. I can get a headache. It is detrimental to my overall health and wellness. I may make reactive choices verses mindful choices. My amygdala may get over-reactive. My sympathetic nervous system may go into fight, flight, or freeze mode. Clearly, my mental health can suffer from a lack of self-care. This can be a good indication that it's time for me to pause, take a breath and look towards myself for nurturing. Usually, it's a sign that I need to slow down, say "no" to many obligations, and listen to my body. It's critical that I don't isolate and that I lean into my support system to not feel alone.

Tonglen is a Tibetan practice to help move energy from pain/suffering and open our hearts to compassion for self and others. It's an exercise that can be helpful to remind me that there are many others around the world that are experiencing lack of balance and neglect of self-care. As I breathe in the pain and suffering of others, I can feel where in my body the tightness and tension reside. Then, I can name/identify the feelings and sensations within the body. Next, I exhale the compassion for those in the world experiencing this pain/suffering. I send compassion for those suffering. I visualize myself sending love, energy, and encouragement to take personal time to rest, to nurture themselves, to eat a warm nutritious meal, to forgive themselves, and to remind them of their self-worth to take this time to do so to heal, recharge and repair. In doing this, this practice allows me to connect with others outside myself, feel the pain/suffering and move into compassion for others and ultimately myself as well. It's a mirror. I am not alone in dealing with so many experiences that run me down and put me out of balance with my self-care. It's universal and we are all connected.

There are many opportunities when difficulties and/or adversities arise. This moment can allow me to recognize what in my life is out of balance. Am I working more hours and taking less breaks? Did I get my walk or yoga class in to show up for myself? Have I over booked myself with appointments, social gatherings, etc?

Self-compassion and self-worth are ingredients to self-care. With self-compassion, I don't guilt trip myself if I can't do everything I had on my list, I may have to make less plans with others to be sure I can cultivate personal time to be in peace. My self-worth confirms the importance of my maintenance with my hygiene, rituals for mornings and nights, and making my own choices that support my values and what's important to me. It is the self-love for my true Self. It's honoring myself. It's good to even adjust rituals around seasonal changes and certain times in life like holidays, colder or warmer months, etc. There is nothing selfish about maintaining your personal recovery care. It's delicious when you can have relationships that embrace this!

Time management can be a challenge. For me, my mornings are my best times to journal, reflect, walk/meditate/exercise, water/meal prep for the day, and set goals for the day. My mind tends to be clear in the mornings. Although, others may find that evenings are their best times to do for self. It depends on schedule, lifestyle, and body.

The key to ongoing, active recovery is to build a resilient mindset that when there are challenges and obstacles with our goals and plans, it's time to get creative and look towards alternatives to stay focused on what's most important to you. This is once again a day to day, inside job. It's work, but it yields the feelings of honoring the Self which leads to higher self-compassion, self-love, and worth. As I practice this more for Self, I can share these intentions with others genuinely.

As I lean more into my true Self and be present with who I truly am, I begin to peel the layers of the past that don't serve me. I get to continue to mentally, physically and spiritually write the next chapters of my life story. I get to heal and recover from PTSD/trauma/mental health issues. I build onto my tools to help guide me when it arises again. There is no linear process to recovery. It's being aware, awake, and humble to accept and move forward.

It's non-negotiable to maintain balance with self-care. It's a key to success in the continuum of any recovery. Flare ups can happen to anyone. We have a lot of external circumstances that we can't control. That is why time management is important to devote time to recharge your battery to include adequate rest, nutrition, ritual/habits that nurture your mind, body and spirit when you wake up in the morning and time before you go to bed. Remember that it's a process and doesn't have to be perfect. It won't be perfect. It can get messy and that's all okay and quite normal. It is the compassion for our self that gets us closer and closer to who we aspire to be, our true Self.

> *To keep the body in good health is a duty...otherwise we shall not be able to keep our mind strong and clear.*
> *~Buddha*

Reflection Questions:
What obstacles arise to your time management for self-care?

When there is a neglect of your self-care, how are your choices impacted to think clearly?

If you were to practice Tonglen, what kind of intention would you like to gift to those suffering/and or in pain?

How can you relate and even connect to the universal suffering/pain in the world?
What areas in your life feel out of balance?

What are some self-care activities that can help re-balance you?

What are some ways to express and show more self-compassion in order to heal?

#16
LETTING GO OF ATTACHMENTS

It's not a matter of letting go - you would if you could.
Instead of "Let it go" we should probably say "Let it be".

~Jon Kabat - Zinn

Attachments are usually the holding on to of sentiments, feelings, possessions, belongings, pride, ego, others and their feelings. It can be painful to lose or let go, especially if our grip is firmly holding onto and not letting it flow.

In the Buddhist approach, non-attachment is a way of life. In sanskrit, non-attachment is called 'aparagrapha'. It is part of the universal moralities of how to interact with self and others. Buddha said, "The root of suffering is attachments." This is a mindfulness practice that takes patience, forgiveness, and much self-compassion and self-care. It is a nonjudgmental approach to circumstances, including ourself.

In western civilization, I had a perspective that attachments to people, the way I feel about others (especially in relationships), my gifts/possessions, my successes, how others viewed me, my reputation, etc were a normal way of life. It was loyalty, endearing, respectful, and almost like my own rigid code of ethics. Pride and ego became a driving force for my choices. I had no idea that I was progressively building opinions towards others and myself of what was right, wrong, good, bad, and had almost no room for the middle.

Attachments to feelings, possessions, outcomes, others, etc. can, like any addiction, manifest into a progressive, unhealthy, painful, confusing and chaotic lifestyle. It develops into a vicious cycle of ups and downs. My peace and happiness can be sacrificed depending on what happens exteriorly. If I don't get my way or feel wronged, my energy, thoughts, and choices can go south and pretty quickly. I suffer. There can be a sense of hopelessness and my sympathetic nervous system is activated. My breathing becomes less cleansing, my body can tense to the stress, energy can get trapped in the body, and my victim state gets awakened in the amygdala part of my brain, especially with hysterical trauma/PTSD.

I am no longer present. I have escaped from my true Self, my internal home in my heart. I stray from listening to myself as to what I need and prevent the act of giving to myself what I need. It's like I've become the back-seat driver, the horn is honking, and I can't even hear my own thoughts. Now that's stressful and dangerous!

Patterns of attachments and control can become our doors to freedom and recovery. It can be our conscious awareness of what universally shows up where we are stuck. In a nonjudgmental way, it can awaken the 'middle path'. This process is the opposite of numbing. It is awakening the pain/suffering. It allows an opportunity to look towards ourselves for relief and recovery. This takes courage, honesty, and clarity of the mind. If I'm staying busy, not taking care of myself, impaired from substances, etc., this can become an obstacle to the new pathway opening in my brain.

Don't fret. Initially it will feel awkward and discomforting. "Trust the process." Honor your process. I can observe and recognize what I'm powerless over. I can surrender to something greater than myself in loving kindness. This is not defeat. This can lead to a glorious long-term sustainable victory in life and recovery. The energy with resistance loses power. Stay focused on you, your true self. The cycle can be broken right here with this clarity. It's a mindful process. It is honoring my grief and honoring myself.

Thich Nhat Hanh says, "Darling I am there for you. Darling I know you are here and I'm very happy. Darling I know you suffer and that is why I'm here for you. Darling I suffer, please help."

These mantras/phrases can be reminders to look towards self and others with an open heart. Compassion for others and self can be difficult especially when someone has wronged me. The goal is peace, recovery internally and inner peace. If I face my problems with others with pride, hate, and judgment, I block my heart to not just others but ultimately myself. This can become dangerous as this is energy and carries weight in the body.

The 'middle path' has balance and space for compassion. It allows less attachments to the outcomes. This process allows openness to many doors and perspectives. In my heart, I place the focus back on myself with kindness, wholeness, and breath. I can allow myself to process what arises in my body and mind if I get charged with a circumstance that feels painful or discomforting. Instead of looking outwards, attempting to "control" exterior people/surroundings and placing blame, anguish or hate towards others or self, I go inward and connect with my spirit, my heart, and that place inside that holds a sacred space of wellness, safety, purity, love, and peace. It's there and it yearns for my return. It awaits me and I forget it doesn't forsake me.

I pause, breathe and allow my own energetic breath to find that space/place in my heart. It is a disservice to escape if I'm trying to awaken my heart. I tell myself to "Come back and lean into yourself, your heart."

Self-study is mindfulness and in the eightfold path this is called 'Svadyaya.' Learning about my attachments, control issues, and how I respond to these moments can bring me opportunities to learn more about my ego and true self. With self-compassion, I can recognize, allow the feelings, investigate how I respond and what I say to myself when I feel this way, and how do I nurture myself. This can become a new program in the brain. My neurological pathways in my brain through practice become stronger with consistency. This is conditioning the brain to respond verses react. It's like muscle memory. It gets stronger!

Reflection Questions:
What are some of your own attachments?

Have you judged yourself or others? In what ways? How does that make you feel when you judge yourself or others?

Do you have any unhealthy patterns that backfire on your true Self?

In what ways have you tried to escape your discomfort?

What are some self nurturing things you can do to calm your system?
What are you powerless over?

How can you surrender and trust the process?

What do you need when you face the pain/suffering from the powerlessness? (For example, self-compassion, self-care, a walk, talk with a supportive person you trust, go to a meeting, pause and breathe)

How can you transform your pain/suffering into the 'middle path' approach?

Are there any areas of your life that can benefit you to do some self-study with compassion?

Imagine you are reprogramming your brain consistently to allow more helpful approaches to pain/suffering. Describe how that would feel to have more mastery of your healthy lifestyle with choices and self-care when facing discomfort?

#17

FINDING PASSION IN LOSSES/GRIEF

What hurts you, blesses you.

Darkness is your candle.

~Rumi

Losses and grief come from painful experiences that we all face in life. Examples of situations that bring pain and suffering are a death of a loved one, an absent parent, a divorce/relationship breakup, health issues, financial losses, legal issues, mental health issues, traumatic events, separation from family, or a national crisis/disaster, etc.

Helen Keller said, "When one door of happiness closes, another opens; but often we look so long at the closed door that we do not see the one which has been opened for us." I remember picking up her book in elementary school and was so inspired by her story. She was blind, deaf and mute and became a social worker for the blind, invented grail, and became an advocate for the blind. Helen had every reason and excuse to give up. Instead, she converted her pain/suffering into something that would serve and inspire millions of people then and now. She has impacted the world in so many positive ways.

Victor Frankl said, "When we are no longer able to change a situation, we are challenged to change ourselves." I remember in my master's program for mental health counseling, I instantly connected with his writings. I learned that he was a neurologist, psychiatrist, and Nazi concentration camp survivor. Existential psychotherapy and Frankl's 'Logotherapy' inspired me to find purpose and meaning even through painful experiences.

My grandmother, "mi abuelita" coming to move in with us at age 4 when my parents separated was one of the greatest gifts in my life. I had no idea that learning Spanish would help me have the leverage to later accelerate in my career. I feel more grounded in my ethnicity knowing that I understand not only the culture, but also the language. Looking back, I had some of the best times in my life with my grandmother. We became like best friends. We laughed watching shows like *Sanford and Son*. She encouraged me to do the things that brought me happiness, like art and music. She gave me the best care, nutrition and genuine love with no quid pro quo. She gave from the heart and showed me what unconditional love means. She was spiritual and had a calming energy that I will never forget. I smile thinking of how special of a lady my grandmother will always be to me. As I write this, I look down at my heart and realize I have her blanket covering me and am reminded that her spirit protects me.

Growing up with a parent who had an active alcohol addiction and mental health issues helped me develop the skills of an addiction counselor way before I even knew that would be the direction of my career. When I was offered an internship to become a clinician in training, I was given an opportunity to grow as a counselor and learn more about addiction, neurology of the brain, PTSD, mental health and recovery. The emotional abandonment from being a child of an alcoholic is healing through the compassion I have developed in understanding the neurobiological components of addiction. Working in this field, has allowed me to have less judgement over others and myself.

Finding my passions through my losses/grief has allowed me to see the other doors that have been opened. Through what I had no control over growing up, I decided to allow my losses and grief experiences to help me become an advocate for those who suffer from addiction. It's rewarding to walk alongside someone who struggles with addiction and offer mentorship, guidance, encouragement, and hope. It is an honor to help those in need when facing addiction. I don't turn my back to the people who deal with this situation. I respect the nature and power addiction has over others' mind, spirit and soul. I like to guide others to their true Self and to remind people who they are, verses, what happened to them with loving kindness and deep compassion.

My career as an addiction counselor has allowed me to grow, heal and see some people awaken to heal. I have made some dear friends from being involved in the addiction and recovery field. I never knew that I could build a successful business and take care of myself financially and comfortably. Continuing my personal recovery work and teaching yoga at a treatment facility has helped me move even more energy and be present with my body, spirit and mind. I have been awakened to allow my creative side to open up and have space in my heart to grow consistently. I look forward to allowing more passions to blossom through my experiences in life. I'm beyond grateful for all my experiences, including the tough times, because these experiences helped me find meaningful purpose and passion in my life. The Universe works in mysterious ways. This is an example of "trusting the process."

Reflection Questions:
Like Helen Keller, do you have other doors in your life? If yes, what are your other doors?

Like Victor Frankl, how have some of your pain/suffering experiences brought you closer to your strengths?

What changes did you make with your circumstances to help you become who you are today?

Can you find purpose and meaning even through your painful experiences?

What are some of your passions?

What are some of your purposes in life?

How would it feel to convert some of your toughest times into light?

#18

KEEP COMING BACK, WORKING YOUR PROGRAM

It does not matter how slowly you go
as long as you do not stop.
~Confucius

Active recovery is ongoing. I stress that this isn't a linear process. It's easy to forget and beat myself up if I have a setback. It's not *if* I will have a setback. It's more like *when* I have a setback, I will come back to my recovery. It's like my mind is saying, "NOW WHAT?!" and then I pause and get back on track with my recovery behaviors to move forward. There are some days that are easier than others. Some days will run smoothly, and some days will be difficult. There is no perfect ending as it is merely the present tense that keeps recovery alive.

Coming back to my support group, healthy activities, cleansing breathing, healthy tools, walks/exercise/yoga, rest, self-compassion, and scheduling time for me and my self-care are all ingredients for maintaining optimum mental health. There is nothing selfish about scheduling time to charge your own battery. If I don't, I suffer, and my choices aren't as clear minded. This is an inside job that no one can do but myself. It is a choice even if that means I ask for support.

I am worthy of recovering from any painful experience.

In 12 steps, we say "keep coming back". I work the 12 steps over and over again. I can be a beginner even after many years. This is okay and quite normal. Similar to yoga, I can be experienced and even find a beginner's class challenging. It's giving myself permission to allow the mistakes without judgment. It's knowing that this is my practice, my own unique journey, and there is no comparison as to what is right and what is wrong. This is the 'middle path' the yin and the yang of my recovery has many perspectives and that is welcomed. It's loving kindness to self when there is hardship. It's honoring when I need to slow down and rest. It's listening when my back hurts. It's pausing when I'm hesitant to give what I don't have for myself to others. It's standing up for myself even if it causes another to get upset. I'm really great about compassion for others. I know self-compassion is an area I can be more present with to help myself recover from pain and suffering. How I talk to myself during periods of setbacks are important to hear.

In Sanskrit, ahimsa (do no harm to self and others) is important to remember when working on recovery. I am mindful of doing no harm through my own actions, words, and my thoughts. I make a list of things I can do once I pause that honor, love and respect myself.

In my eightfold yoga teacher training, my mentor said, "look forward to emotional abandonment, and look towards yourself!" It took me a while to absorb and interpret this perspective. After thinking about this, it made sense as to not resist my fears but embrace them and look towards myself to comfort, recover and not freeze, fight or flight. Emotional abandonment is a hysterical and historical event for me. My story has gotten me stuck in that part of my brain. If I pause and allow the feelings to surface and then look towards myself, I then start to be present and see that my past is not who I am and does not define me.

It's like this is an opportunity to be present and say to myself, when this feeling arises, "I can do for me what I need to feel safe, loved, nurtured and secure." This awareness is a mindful practice allowing my inner child to heal what I didn't know or couldn't process as a four-year-old. I have the answers in me to help myself recover and I smile. It's embracing both sides and getting to know them both. It's the opposite of hoping something will never happen. It's spending time and energy in loving kindness for my self recovery and self-compassion.

Working my recovery program can be a creative process. It can be a time to do the things for myself that I wish I had time for but did other things instead. It is a time to say no to others and say yes more to me. It's making my self-care luxurious, relaxing, fun, and innovative. It's about self-discovery and self-compassion. It's developing a personal plan for the 'NOW WHAT?' moments when they happen. It's looking inward for healing and connecting with nature and those that are supportive in my recovery process.

I can take an Epsom salt bath, take a walk, drink a cup of tea/hydrate with water and lemon, take a cat nap, read, sit at the table and enjoy a nutritious meal, massage my hands and feet, take a day off from work, do yoga, meditate, etc. I can schedule and keep my art date with myself with no excuses! The gifts of connection come from sharing and having awareness of different perspectives. Gratitude helps bring back our intention.

> When struggling, borrowing hope from others can strengthen your mindset in recovery.

Coming back to your own practice, your own program, and honoring where you are brings gifts by healing the hole in the heart, one breath at a time, one minute at a time, and one day at a time.

Reflection Questions:
What kinds of routines do you have in place to help self-care on a consistent basis? Write them down.

What fears do you have presently? What can you do for yourself to recover when those fears arise?

Are there any opportunities to look towards yourself for self-care? If yes, what can you do for yourself?

Are there any self-care practices that you would like to do for yourself right now?

Do you have support for your recovery from others, like a group or program?

Would you include yourself as part of your support system as well?

#19

MODERATION - MORE PLEASE! WHEN IS ENOUGH, ENOUGH?

Everything that exceeds moderation
has an unstable foundation.
~Seneca

Moderation is a term described as avoidance of excess or extreme behaviors and finding a middle ground. The ability to moderate in certain areas for some (a lot of us) can be quite challenging. There are behaviors that can develop into addiction. With this in mind, behaviors like being on the internet, alcohol/drug use, tobacco, caffeine, sugar, working long hours, perfectionism, codependency, sex, shopping, etc. can progress into compulsive behaviors. This progression can develop in anyone depending on choices. When I'm not conscious and clear minded, my choices can be influenced negatively. This can prevent my ability to tap into my clear executive thinking and decision making. Many eastern philosophies stress the importance of the purity of the mind and body to make conscious, awakened decisions that impact the outcome of my life. That is why a mindfulness practice can help regulate the awareness when I've ventured into an extreme zone. With just about anything, "Moderation is key."

> Be moderate to taste the joys of life in abundance.
> ~Epicurus

Working in the addiction field for over twenty years, I have learned that there is no discrimination on who can sway away from moderation. I see EVERYONE. Parents, grandparents, clergy, teachers, attorneys, physicians, carpenters, painters, staff at a restaurant, students, nurses, military, etc. all have been through my doors. Many of these people are kindhearted, responsible, hardworking, and family oriented people. When someone gets arrested from driving while impaired (DWI), often there are stigmas. Unfortunately, some people attach themselves to the negative stories that came from their impairment and feel less worthy because of this.

> When impaired, you simply won't make the same choices. That's not a reflection of who you truly are.

Impairment and a lack of moderation can be deadly/dangerous, costly, embarrassing, and very painful. It can pull us away from our true Self and even feed our ego. I have often observed that it's like seeing people sleepwalking through their life with no conscious connection to their own senses and levels of moderation.

I see how western culture can almost glorify excess and extreme. The nature of tolerance makes me less sensitive to a substance or activity. When my physical tolerance is going up, my mental tolerance doesn't increase at the same rate by comparison. So, it makes sense for me to go more by how I feel to determine when I have had enough. I used to think having a higher tolerance is an ability but it's more like having a liability because it actually tricks me into believing that I am 'handling it."

For example, I love me some coffee! In the mornings, I look forward to that warm cup of coffee. The smell makes me smile. It's like a ritual first thing. After college, I developed a liking towards Starbucks® coffee. A friend of mine introduced me to a red eye cup of coffee. It's a cup of coffee with a shot of espresso. It's essentially like having a double. My tolerance to caffeine had developed into a record high. My physical tolerance shot through the roof and I didn't think of it as being any big deal. In my mind, I'm like "I'm handling this." Then, I wanted one cup for lunch and one in the evening after dinner. I was thinking that this was helping me be productive and I could get all my stuff done. It was amazing! If I got a headache (withdrawal) or felt low in energy, I could do it again and again and again. Well, one day I was going in for my regular doctors' checkup. When my primary doctor checked my heart, he was very concerned by my high heart rate. He even sent me to a specialist as he was concerned of my family history with heart disease and my rapid heart rate while still being in his office. Anyways, I switched over to decaf coffee for many years as this experience awakened me to see that I wasn't moderating very well. For me, it took an extreme situation to make me make changes.

Tolerance can go down through choices and it can pick up through my choices as well. Once I have developed tolerance to one thing, it's easy to progress in my tolerance once I bring it back into my life. I know caffeine for me is one of those substances that seems harmless, yet I know it has its cons if not moderated.

Towards the end of my eight-fold path yoga teacher training, I wanted to deepen my meditation practice. I started to observe my morning routine with coffee and how my mind felt focused (on a lot of things) and my body at times was jumpy from the caffeine induced energy. Relaxing the mind and body and being present was a bit more challenging. In meditation, I allowed my mind to race, thinking of all I would be doing that day or what thoughts were occupying my mind. It was like being on speed. Calming the mind, slowing the mind, letting go of any tension in the body, and relaxing into a state of peace are all benefits from meditation that I was missing out on because of my overuse of caffeine at the time.

I decided to do a liver detox with a group of my yoga friends from class. I was thinking, 'I can do anything for ten days.' Well, I learned very quickly that withdrawal from caffeine is no joke! I had a headache for three long days. My body felt sluggish. My mind/brain felt like it wasn't connecting my thoughts clearly and as quickly. I would wake up and think "I can just fall asleep and rest." My body was acting like it was in a bit of a shock. I can see why there is a coffee shop on every corner in town. The various coffee and energy drinks are like staples for many of us.

After months of no caffeine, my meditation practice felt deeper and calmer. On the liver detox, I lowered my sugar intake as well. I went more inward and felt my senses repairing. My senses weren't numb anymore. Looking back, I enjoyed this process as I journaled and became more aware of how my senses can lead me to a stronger spiritual practice to heal, grow, and become enlightened. Since then, I am modifying my lifestyle for more balance in areas that I feel out of balance more. It's a practice that takes compassion, awareness, and forgiveness.

All in all, having a higher tolerance is dangerous. It tricks me to believe I'm okay and I do more. My physical body adapts, and the strength and clarity of my senses go down. My mental tolerance doesn't increase at the same rate of my physical tolerance. My choices become more driven from my physical tolerance. My progression with my vice can develop and it can affect my mental, physical and spiritual wellness.

Reflection Questions:
Do you have a higher tolerance to anything?

How has your tolerance tricked you into believing you're okay?

In what ways have you thought your tolerance was beneficial?

Have you had any withdrawals from coming off a substance? (Some examples of withdrawals are irritability, anxiousness, restlessness, cravings, etc.)

Are there any habits/rituals that you would like to abstain from and become more conscious with your mind, body and spirit connection?

Do you have a support group that can help with this process?

What are some other healthy habits/rituals you could replace your vice with?

#20

THE GIFT OF SHARING

PERSONAL STORIES

Daring greatly means the courage to be vulnerable, it means to show up and be seen, to ask for what you need, to talk about what you are feeling, and to have the hard conversations.

~Brene' Brown

Sharing personal stories brings gifts like bonding/connection, empathy, listening to another, love, honor, hope, inspiration, respect, and humility. When I think of the lyrics of some songs it brings connection. People can relate and feel what the song may mean to them. Many song writers say that the words and stories come straight from their heart. When sharing straight from the heart, it's an automatic story telling time and the listener feels a part of the story through the feelings that we can relate to one another. It can be a creative transformation moving pain into gifts. It is a form of art.

The connection that comes from sharing is timeless, meaning that there are some songs, poems, "ted talks", books, interviews, etc. that every time you may hear/read you can relate, connect and feel inspired to move through whatever obstacle(s) you may be facing. Willie Nelson wrote the song, *Crazy* and Patsy Cline sang this song. No matter when, where, or what's going on, when I hear this song, I feel heartache, love without limits, pain from loving another, and disappointment. I can both relate to and feel the song deeply.

Music and storytelling can evoke a place in our heart that senses another's pain. That is empathy. It's like I know in my gut that Willie Nelson and Patsy Cline understand the pain from a broken heart. They get this and have been down this road before. I feel this through the music. Some of the best sharing for me has been when another person shares what they have been through and what they are doing and/or have done to overcome and grow. This is inspiring and gives me hope.

Sharing personal stories can bring up different emotions, feelings and thoughts. There are many opinions and perspectives on sharing stories, especially personal stories. It can feel like stepping out of our comfort zone. It takes courage and much self-compassion.

Confidentiality, safety, and trust are key in ensuring a sacred space. The stories in our mind that bring pain and suffering are usually historical. "If it's hysterical, it's historical." When I say historical, I mean that the story has a past connection to the heart. This phrase stuck in my head after a yoga training with Nikki Myers. There is energy and attachments to what has happened in the past. This energy can get lodged in the body. How I feel when I tell that story can help awaken me to better identify the area in my body I want to heal. It can bring much chemical charge and what I do with this energy is important. The key is to move the energy and story into a place that keeps me from getting stuck in a repetitive cycle in my pain body.

As a treatment group facilitator, I have a guideline that stresses the importance of confidentiality. The best groups that I have participated in are the groups that offer sharing. "You can't heal what you don't own." The self-disclosure and sharing can, over a period of time, lesson the strength of the power the story has over us. This brings more emotional freedom.

For me, it helps me see where I have attached who I am with the story. This is an illusion as what happened isn't who I am. Detaching with love, honoring my grief, and connecting with others who show empathy can allow me to gain strength in my recovery. Also, I realize many others around the world have experienced this or are experiencing this right now. I am not alone!

Tonglen in Buddhism helps me reconnect with my intention and spiritual author Eckhart Tolle, contends that old emotional pain is carried around inside a person in something he calls a "pain-body," which loves using emotions to control our thinking. So, if I am in my 'pain body' and think of others who may be in their pain body, I visualize and connect in my heart the feeling of empathy and what I would want to gift the other. With someone with a broken heart, I would want to give them love, no judgement, kindness, listening, maybe, if appropriate, laughter, honor, hope, gratitude, etc. The moment I send that energy to another, I evoke that space and place in my heart and give to myself those gifts as well. I mirror the love to the other and to myself. "I can't give what I don't have inside." The connection with another and sharing is medicine to the soul. For me, it's life transforming. It's a reminder of the phrase, "let it begin with me." Recovery and humility are a beautiful thing.

In Al-Anon®, I had an opportunity to share my story with my home group. It felt safe to share as I have heard many of these people share their own story of what had initially brought them there. Al-Anon® for me has helped me develop a better relationship with myself. The program steps help me get unstuck when I feel charged from my story and am reminded of the areas that bring the source of pain and suffering. How I choose to respond can either harm me or help me. It is staying focused on my personal recovery/self-care and my true Self, no matter what!

There are risks when sharing. The risks can bring up trust/safety, ego, and shame/guilt issues. Blocking the sharing can prevent opportunities for healing. Repressing intense feelings through numbing can lead to progressive emotions that continue to energetically get lodged in our tissues/bodies. Over a period of time, dis-ease in the mind, body and spirit can progress, creating more havoc in our system. Examples of problems that develop can be depression, low self-esteem, self-medication/numbing for short term relief, isolation, self-sabotaging behaviors, anger, various addictions, heightened fears, sense of hopelessness, loneliness, victim feeling, blaming others, scarcity mentality, codependency, sleep issues, separation from our true Self, lack of self worthiness, distrust, and various 'stinking thinking', etc.

In Y12SR® yoga (a recovery-based yoga), we say "the issues live in our tissues." The first half of the yoga class, the yoga teacher is called the space holder to allow those attending to share regarding topics of recovery and the second part of yoga class is to bring in Asanas (postures), and Pranayama (breathing exercises). This experience is a process that allows the movement to help wring out the tissues so that the issues can flow out of us. Facilitating groups as well as being a student of these practices has given me many gifts of hope, strength, and gratitude.

There are gifts from the risks of sharing as well. Some of the biggest gifts people have given me are from the moments they have shared from their heart a personal story that makes me realize that I am not alone. They understand and/or can relate to me. We are connected. Stories can feel messy and beautiful at the same time. The story can lose its power over me as I release the shame/guilt.

Bottom line, recovery takes looking not just towards myself but also to the connection with others. It is opening up, with safety, that place that hurts inside our heart. It's allowing the negative energy, 'the infection' to have a chance to breathe, have time to heal, and recover. It isn't perfect. It's about progress and being open to active recovery. This is a continuum process that has no start and no finish line. It's maintaining optimum care and awakening my mind. It is the opposite of staying busy, numbing, and solely looking outside myself. My self-care is non-negotiable as I know that my active recovery is what has saved me from many times going down the rabbit hole of my 'pain body' and mind. It is through sharing and listening to others who I can relate to that reinforces that I'm on the path that I want to be on. Onward and forward here I come! It feels good. I am worthy. I am whole. I am healing. We are all connected.

Reflection Questions:
Are there areas in your life that you feel stuck? Where in your body do you hold that stress and tension?

Have you ever been inspired by another person through their sharing a personal story and experience? In what ways did it bring inspiration and/or motivation to you?

Do you have stories that are historical that can bring hysterical feelings when charged from an experience and/or situation? If so, what is the story?

How would you like to move into new chapters of your story to help bring peace in your soul?

What would it feel like being able to move the energy of your story from your 'pain body' and mind into a safer and healing space of growth and transformation?

How have others sharing their stories gifted their hope, strength, and resiliency to you? What can this teach you to help you move into your recovery?

Can you borrow hope and strength from others even if you don't feel it yet?

In your gut, do you have a story that brings shame/guilt still and that a safe place to share could be beneficial if you know that you are in a 'judgement free zone?' Would you like a trusted counselor, friend, or recovery group to add to your support?

What obstacles and/or fears do you experience when thinking of sharing your story?

What does hope look like to you?

#21
BUILDING SUPPORT

Once a person is determined to help themselves,
there is nothing that can stop them.
~Nelson Mandela

Support is the holding up of our structural foundation. It keeps us from falling down or collapsing mentally, physically and/or spiritually. In active recovery, building support from others and with ourselves is essential for an optimal continuum of mindful wellness. A strong support system can strengthen the foundation of my personal recovery.

I struggle with asking for support at times. Owning a business, I forget that it is okay to ask another counselor to help me, get extra help with phone calls, paperwork, mentorship, therapy, education, and computer, technology help. It's taken difficult moments in my life like getting sick, burnt out, and even death in the family to push me to get more support. When I'm not actively working on my recovery from perfectionism, workaholism, codependency, obsessive compulsiveness, etc., I end up pushing myself to exhaustion. I don't think clearly. I end up beating myself up for feeling like a failure. This is something I call "stinking thinking." It affects my appetite, sleep, mental health and self-esteem. There is nothing serving me with this mindset.

Awakening to shift my thoughts and look towards myself for self-compassion is like allowing my energy to flow through me in a healing, positive way. It's an awareness of listening to my body with no shame and guilt. It's a reminder to honor myself and pause and take a cleansing breath. When I am actively practicing self-compassion, I don't wait until I'm in a breaking moment to ask for help. I embrace the gifts from feeling more balanced, which include better rest, less stress, practicing more habits and rituals that serve me, and an expanding sense of self-worth.

I realize that my perfectionistic ways of thinking only separate me from my true self. I set myself up for failure if I'm not in my mindful space to humbly embrace the beauty of connection and asking for support. This view reminds me that asking for help and support is a part of my self-care. It is actually the opposite of weakness for me as "I'm healing and I'm not alone." I learn more about what I need for support and who is a part of my support. I am more honest with myself with loving kindness to open my path for growth. It's an exploration and learning process getting to know myself deeper.

Support can be in different forms. There is support from others. There is support from myself. Both are equally important to strengthen success. For me, I'm always open to building my support. This isn't a linear process for me. It evolves and expands depending on what I'm doing and how I'm feeling. Part of my external support are my neighbors, my yoga friends/family, my Al-Anon® friends/family, my family, my friends, my creative art farmers market buddies, my fur babies, colleagues, my spiritual friends, nature/outdoors, my leisure activities that are uplifting to my spirit, etc. I am learning more about strengthening and building my internal support.

I make more time for myself to go on a walk, to write and read, art/creative time, time for meditation consistently, time for feasting on my nutrition, taking time to pause and connect with my breath, rest when I'm tired, saying no more, take a bath, making gifts, create more, having quiet time and enjoying more of my own company. My own internal support becomes a form of expression. It's like creating your own painting of what makes you feel good. This development is sustainably healing when I keep coming back to building more kinds of support with an open heart and a whole lot of compassion.

Building true support is like building a sustainable home. I build onto my foundation so that it's strong. I add external and internal support to help add on to the foundation. As I add more support, I maintain my internal home. I sustain through storms and have help to put things back together when there are moments of chaos and repair needs. I do this with grace and acceptance most days. When I struggle, feel tired, or feel lost, I ask for help from someone who is actually doing it and/or are succeeding in their goal. Research says if I have at least three people who are attaining their goal and I am working on a similar goal, the support from these people can help strengthen my personal goals. In my experience, it helps knowing that I'm not alone and realizing that the ups and downs are all a part of the process. I start to focus on my gratitude from the support of others in my life and my gratitude for the time that I take to honor myself through my grief.

Reflection Questions:
What does support look like to you?

Who is a part of your support network?

How do you look towards yourself for support?

In what ways has your support network helped in previous times in your life?

What are some ways to build both internal and external support for optimal recovery?

What are your gratitudes?

#22

DISMANTLING THE EGO AND CONNECTIONS TO TRUE SELF

Your ego is not your amigo.
~Unknown

Ego is a false sense of my self-identity. It can bring attachments to possessions, relationships, and desires. Illusions in the mind can be created. I can get further from my true self. Ego comes in different forms like my pride, what I do, what I own, what/whom I control, etc. This lifestyle can create pain and suffering.

> *When the ego dies, the soul awakens.*
> *~Buddhist teaching*

Like nature, there is an impermanence in my true Self. There are changes and evolving flows of life. My soul awakens as I detach myself from my ego. There is no judgement. There is an expanding space full of compassion. There are moments of contraction. Contraction is a normal process that is sacred. It is a time to be present and allow the body to process the energy. Moments of contraction are essential for spurts of expansion. In all of us, there are transformations that have the ebb and flow of nature. There is a healthy empty space in the soul.

In my garden, there is a beautiful white camellia tree. It blooms a gorgeous white flower in colder months of the year. Once the flower blooms, it lasts for a few days. The petals start to change colors and they eventually will fall to the ground. In summer months, the camellia is green with no flowers. There is a beautiful nature about this plant as it's always transforming. There are moments of expansion when the blooms are all at its peak. There are moments of contraction when in the summer its blooms are dormant. I can relate to the impermanence of the camellia plant that I have admired for over 15 years. I ask myself, "How can I view my true self more like the camellia?"

Finding ways that serve our true nature can bring more happiness and long-term recovery. Some rituals to detach from our egos and awaken our true self are forgiveness and letting go, honesty/openness, surrendering the need to control, enjoying silent moments with self, and reflecting on gratitude. This leads to a quality of life that has more peace and serenity.

Reflection Questions:
How has my ego tricked me?

What kind of attachments have I developed from being in my ego mind?

How can detaching from my ego and connecting more to my true self help me?

What part of your soul longs for your awakening?

What are some rituals/habits that can help you awaken your true self? What are ways to surrender the ego?

Is there anything in nature that you can relate to that brings spirituality and beauty in the impermanent nature of being? Please describe.

#23
GRIEF, PAIN, &
BROKENNESS

*There is no way around grief and loss: you can dodge
all you want, but sooner or later you just have to go into
it, through it, and, hopefully, come out the other side.
The world you find there will never be the same as the
world you left.*

~Johnny Cash

Grief is a normal feeling that occurs after a tragedy, loss, or an experience that can bring a sense of powerlessness. These moments can bring pain. Losses and grief can come in waves. There can be moments that feel horrific and some moments that feel slightly better. This can happen over and over again. It can be like lightning bolts. There are many stages of grief. There is no right or wrong way to do this. How I respond to grief can help me recover and heal.

In Tonglen, when I see others in pain from grief, I send them my kindest thoughts to suffer less and to honor their grief. I offer support through listening with no judgement. I share my own heart and empathy. I can relate to the common theme in life of losses and grief. I am learning more to embrace that life has many uncertainties and impermanence. I wish for others a chance to find meaning in their losses and to look towards other doors. This practice brings honor in my own grief and helps me recognize that I'm not alone.

> *Grief is like the ocean; it comes in waves ebbing and flowing. Sometimes the water is calm, and sometimes it is overwhelming. All we can do is learn to swim.*
> *~Vicki Harrison*

Through counseling, I can see how easy it is to get stuck with my attachments to my losses. When my grandmother passed, I was saddened, hurt, felt guilty to not be there and to have not seen her before she had a heart attack, and I was confused as to if she was okay. There was a rush of emotions and it was so confusing to process at age 18. I had lost not just my grandmother, but I had lost the dearest friend in my life. I lost the person who I trusted more than anything. She was like the person who I could feel loved by no matter what. She was my safety. When she passed, it was all too much, and I was more than overwhelmed. I felt alone, pained, and had a hard time accepting what I had no control over. I was away my freshman year of college and already feeling the separation from my home and family. So, during that time, it felt like I reopened a wound I didn't even know I had.

When I lost my father, it was even more confusing. I felt sad, relieved, a sense of bitter sweetness, shame, anger, confusion, and a deep emptiness in my heart. I felt I carried a lot of unfinished grief that progressed from a young age with my father and that made my grief process feel amplified. I felt a hole in my heart. My father passed approximately four years after my grandmother. Once again, his passing felt like salt had been poured on a deep wound from within.

During the four years of two major losses in my life, I had just moved back to my hometown and was on my own. I also had a traumatic arm injury that took multiple surgeries to recover from. It was a compound fracture which was a major setback in my life. I had to pause my education and when I returned to school, I was in much physical pain. I was prescribed opiates and some moments even hooked up to a morphine pump. Also, I was laid off work while my father was dying of cancer. "When it rains, it pours!" Needless to say, I was beyond devastated.

> Sometimes it's OK if the only thing you did today was breathe.
> ~Yumi Sakugawa

Having my life experiences, I can now truly see how anyone could develop addictions. It becomes so easy to fill the hole/space in the heart and to numb or pause the pain from deep within. Whether it's an unhealthy relationship, staying busy, drinking and drugging, codependency, etc. they all can develop into forms of unhealthy habits that temporarily numb the pain, but it is no long-term solution. If anything, it seemed like I was stuck with a lot of shame and guilt. I experienced moments that I had no choice but to lean into my physical and emotional pain. There was no escape and it kept showing back up, like an uninvited guest. As much as I wanted to say goodbye to it and never have it come back again, I could not see, at the time, that the Universe was wanting me to find more compassion for myself and others. All I could think was 'why is this happening again?'

I had so much negative energy and feelings all bottled up inside me. My energy had been trapped in my tissues and this became a normal habit. Thinking about my losses and all the things I had no control over felt unbearable at times. It came in waves. One day I was doing better and another day I felt defeated. I had no idea where to even start or what to do to recover. Looking back, the more I avoided the feelings of grief, the more I would find myself in situations with other experiences that reminded me of more loses, grief, and pain. Subconsciously, I would involve myself in relationships with unclear boundaries and codependency. This was a vicious cycle of pain and suffering. I was becoming my harshest critic and my worst enemy.

Eventually, I was attaching myself to my mistakes, what happened, my imperfections, and my low moments in my life. I had no clear concept of self-love and self-compassion. I hadn't developed the tools from counseling, mentorship, 12-step programs, mental health education, various therapies, chiropractic healing, acupuncture, yoga, healthy relationships, and group therapy. I was starting to wonder what was wrong with me and how could I get out of this gloomy place. There were so many times that I felt that I couldn't trust others, myself or the Universe. My brain was in a place that was more in a reactive mode verses me tapping into my part of the brain that could pause and respond with more self-compassion. I hadn't learned about the brain and trauma. There was more struggle not having developed useful coping skills.

It was through my pain and suffering that brought me to ask for and seek out help. I saw my first counselor (who was amazing) and she allowed me to get off my chest what I had buried behind my shame and guilt. She gifted me with empathy, sharing that she too experienced some of the things I had experienced in her own way. She had no judgement. Instead she allowed me to find beauty in my story as I saw beauty and honor in hers. I felt lighter and she allowed me to start my healing process. Through the process of healing my pain, I furthered my education in mental health, addiction recovery, yoga, and holistic healing. I continue to grow my garden of compassion in search of more love and wisdom for myself and others.

Reflection Questions:
What losses have you experienced? Do you have any current losses that pain you now?

Have you seen any patterns in your feelings and thoughts when experiencing losses/grief?

What are your fears? Do you see any relation to your fears from your past losses/grief?

How do you respond and/or react when you experience grief?

Have you experienced any extreme losses and/or grief? (Death in the family, mental/physical abuse, addiction in family, accident, emotional abandonment, combat, separation from family, injury, trauma, etc)

What are some healthy coping skills that can be added to your toolbox to help face uncertainty and/or impermanence?

Do you have a friend, family, counselor, support group, etc. where it is safe to share?

How can you become more compassionate with yourself when facing grief?

How do you honor your grief?

How do you honor yourself when facing grief?

Have you developed compassion and/or passions through your grief?

#24

IT'S ALL A JOURNEY

*I have learned to live my life one step, one breath, and
one moment at a time, but it was a long road. I set out
on a journey of love, seeking truth, peace and
understanding.*
I am still learning.
~Mohammad Ali

Life is a journey. There are moments in the journey
that have beginnings, twist and turns, waiting periods,
repeats, feeling lost, clear and unclear moments,
moments that feel confusing, and endings. There are
many cycles in the journey of life.

There is a place called home inside each one of us.
That place is inside our heart. "Home is where the heart
is." I have heard this phrase before and never really
applied it literally. Our home within each of us is what
we create and what we need for safety, comfort, and love.
We get to be the creators of this space in our heart. It is

your home. Your space. Your own path that heals you. In times of distress, this is a place you can always come back to no matter what is going on in your life.

This space in our heart is built one step at a time, one breath at a time, and one moment at a time. It is a sacred space that we can always return to and invite ourselves into with love, truth, peace, and understanding. This is where the imagination can bring us creativity, expression, and therapy.

> The time will come when, with elation you will greet yourself arriving at your own door, in your own mirror and each will smile at the other's welcome...
> ~From the Poem, 'Love After Love' by Derek Walcott

I say to myself, "Welcome Frances to your home in your heart. This is a place you can relax and be all of you. There is no wrong or right. You can rest, breathe, nurture yourself without any judgement, and take care of yourself." In my home, I have a candle lit that is welcoming me. I watch the flame flicker as I settle more in my heart. I expand my lungs, cleansing my space inside, exhaling anything that no longer serves me. I can breathe. I pause and sit with myself. I don't feel alone in this space. I am protected. It is cozy and calm. This is a spiritual practice that allows me to reflect on the present moment with loving kindness and compassion. I am grateful for this place I can always come home to and rest, quiet the mind and listen to what it is that I need. I look forward to this place in my heart. It has been through my own journey that I found home. My own home that gives me endless self-care.

> *Art is creative for the sake of realization, not for the amusement; for transfiguration, not for the sake of play. It is the quest for our self that drives us along the eternal and never-ending journey we must all make.*
> *~Marc Beckmann*

Reflection Questions:
If you were to create your own home in your heart, describe what this place is like or what would you like it to be like? (Use your imagination!)

Can you see your life as a journey? In what ways have you had beginnings, twists and turns, pausing moments, confusion, feelings of "I'm on track" or "I'm off track", and even endings?

Using your senses, can you describe your home that you are creating inside your heart.

How does it feel?

Are there any textures?

How does it smell?

What do you see?

Are there any tastes, flavors, etc?

Are there any sounds? Or is it quiet? Or any music or sounds of nature?

Draw a picture. (Abstract art is fine.)

#25

BREAKTHROUGH-
RECOVERY WORKS IF YOU
WORK IT AND YOU'RE
WORTH IT

Recovery is not a race. You don't have to feel guilty if it
takes you longer than you thought it would.
~Unknown

Recovery is a concept used in many forms depending on the situation. In addiction, recovery is the work I do to help sustain my long-term balance for my wellness and healing.

It's not linear as it's a continuous process. There are many twists and turns in life with ups and downs. Active recovery is like yoga in the sense that it is a practice that allows me to twist out excess negative energy in my tissues when needed. It's a mindful practice that allows energy that does not serve to me to exit the mind and body instead of repressing my feelings. This becomes a purification ritual much like a ceremonialist/healer who awakens one's inner strengths, other doors, passions, and home in their own heart.

> To keep the body in good health is a duty...Otherwise we shall not be able to keep our mind strong and clear.
> ~Buddha

Self-care isn't selfish. It's a practice that includes what helps me clear my mind. It's giving myself permission to rest when I'm tired. It's fueling/nutrition that gives vitality to my body. I can walk and move when I know I need to move out some energy.

They say in 12 step programs, "Be mindful of people, places and things." If I need to detox myself from environments that bring me down and lower my frequencies, I pay attention and listen to my intuition. I can limit my time or opt to not spend time with those who aren't a positive influence in my life. There are times that I plan my own self-care when I know I will be around those who are disrespectful or impolite. I don't have to please everyone and nor will everyone like me. That's life.

> Surround yourself with people who respect and treat you well.
> ~Claudia Black

Choosing wisely my environments can help me with my recovery. At times, I have to pause, take a deep breath, and I ask myself, "What do I want to do?" and "Do I really want to hang out or do this if my gut needs rest or quietness?" I don't shame or guilt trip myself. The days of people pleasing didn't serve me. I look towards myself for recovery to tune into my own frequency and follow my intuition as to what helps my awareness and consciousness. A word of caution, not everyone will accept this and at times even guilt trip you. I'm learning to take a deep breath and let it go in my exhale. Your recovery is about you and your own journey. This becomes your own art. You are the painter.

> I will tell you what I have learned myself. For me, a long five or six-mile walk helps. And one must go alone and every day.
> ~Brenda Ueland

I'm learning that my recovery involves support from others like Al-Anon®, recovery yoga, and time to connect with myself for personal reflection. I am journal writing more of my thoughts, feelings, habits/patterns, and emotional blocks. Sometimes my walks are mindful meditative practices. I can move energy while I think. I can observe the ebb and flow, distractions, and gratitudes in my mind. I can pause the chaos in my life and nurture my soul.

Walks for me make me feel more alive, healthy, and clearer in my mind. My tissues thank me for this time of self-care. It is a good feeling when I make time for myself to nurture that inner space in my heart. It's an excellent way to allow energy to move out of my system. I have let go of a lot of stuff I don't have control of on walks to the ocean. The waves remind me of the impermanence and beauty of acceptance.

Creating rituals and habits that serve me are important. This is a practice and work that becomes my ongoing assignment to add to my list of self nurturing things I can do to look towards myself for the ongoing recovery process. I am honoring my grief through ongoing recovery practices.

> The life which is not examined is not worth living.
> ~Plato

One day at a time is a practice that allows me to observe and do self-inquiry with no judgement. I get to do more self-study. In yoga, being open to being a student allows me to learn and expand my heart. This process allows me to develop a personal practice for my own wellness. John Holt says, "We learn to do something by doing it. There is no other way."

As they say in yoga, this is a practice. It's a journey not a destination. Recovery is action not just words. Like my mat in yoga, I can gain more optimal healing when I keep coming back, showing up for myself and holding my own back and my own heart one breath at a time. It's recognizing that energy is constantly moving. I cannot afford to not do my work in recovery as I don't want to suffer. I can feel pain. It's up to me to develop and work on my tools to not suffer more than I have already.

Dr. John Murphy states, "Your desire is your prayer. Picture the fulfillment of your desire now and feel its reality and you will experience the joy of the answered prayer." I visualize what I want for myself. I make vision boards regularly to imagine. I think of what brings me joy. I work on focusing what cultivates more joy in my life. I am accepting impermanence more with the intention to find more joy in the NOW.

> Art, you just do it
> ~Martin Roy

Part of my active recovery plan is being creative and finding ways to allow myself to cultivate my joy. Creativity comes in different forms. I practice this with my groups on how to be more creative. My meditation altar and rituals can be creative especially when I'm traveling. The most important thing is to try and do something that helps with your recovery even if it's not perfect. It won't be prefect. That is okay. Self-compassion for me has helped me to better understand the difference between working my recovery verses going back to my old ways that don't serve me or my long-term wellness. Mistakes are normal. Yes, I will keep coming back. Yes, I am worth it! Thank you Al-Anon®, 12 step programs, yoga, nature, and my friends in recovery! I am beyond grateful for the support to heal and recover one day at a time, one breath at a time, and one step at a time.

Reflection Questions:
What are you recovering from?

What do you want from recovery?

How can you create daily/weekly practices for habits/rituals that include your recovery?

Who is inspiring to you that motivates your active personal recovery?

What can interfere with your value of recovering?

How does self-care tie into building strength in your recovery?

Reflecting back, how had not actively engaging in your recovery lead to negative outcomes?

What values do you want to protect?

How can your recovery help with your goals?

#26

DISTRUST - IS IT SAFE?

Trust yourself. You have survived a lot and you will survive whatever is coming.

~Tiny Buddha

Distrust is lack of faith, confidence, and/or reliability on a person or situation. Distrust is a common feeling for some. It is normal to experience this feeling. It's important to practice healthy boundaries to tap into conscious awareness for safety and self-care.

Distrust has brought me many emotions that can trigger a separation from my true self. I begin to tell my old story of being unworthy, unable to trust, it's safer to be alone, etc. If I am not clear minded, I can begin my flight/fight/freeze response and continue to react to the insanity of behaviors that don't serve me. My self-care can take a downward plunge if I am unaware of my mind's thoughts. I can focus on what I have control over verses focusing on what I'm powerless over.

When facing my fears, I can come back to the practice of pausing and taking a cleansing breath. I can be here now. I sit with myself and go inward with deep compassion. I can "offer chaos a cup of tea." I'm not escaping my fears, but instead recognizing, observing, investigating and then with love becoming my best nurturer. This becomes my personal practice to come back to, like my yoga mat. It's honoring the time, space and care I make for myself regardless.

Some yoga practices that I can come back to when I'm feeling an overwhelming sense of distrust can be 2-4 simple postures that feel good to me. There is no right or wrong. It's a chance for me to listen to what I need to heal. I can lay in Savasana (corpse pose) to relax the mind. I can sit in meditation pose to go inward and listen to my body. I can reconnect with my breath and exhale longer, thereby moving the excess energy out that doesn't serve me. I can do alternate nostril breathing to purify and heal my tissues. I can do a body scan and pay attention to where my body is holding tension and focus on moving my breath through these areas to shift my pain into a flow that I can let go. I can visualize my body recovering and feeling alive. This allows me to be present to my own gratitude to practice my self-care especially when I need it the most.

> Don't trust too much. Don't love too much. Don't hope too much.Because that too much can hurt you so much.
> ~Buddhist teachings and science

Approaching trust in a 'middle path' way, can bring more balance. Can you trust and still have space for mistakes? Can you love and still have distance? Can you hope and have space for disappointment? Nothing is perfect. Impermanence happens over again with cycles of life. How can I face trust with more compassion towards self and others? What are some ways to look towards myself for trust? What patterns do I observe looking at distrust?

> This is the gift of meditation practice- we find we can TRUST
> who we most deeply are.
> ~Tara Brach

The great trust for me is showing up for myself in a way that no one else can. It's been through distrust that I have become more awakened to practicing my own self-trust. Instead of judging who is right or wrong and saying "if he/she didn't do/say this, I wouldn't have done/said that!", I pause and go inward to the space I call 'home in my heart.' I nurture myself with trust. Regardless, I can provide internal trust to myself through that "I love you and I will not forsake you" part of myself.

This moment can bring an energy shift. That power struggle, negativity and hate can't win. That suffering doesn't win. I can recognize what hurts in me and others. I can allow myself to feel. I can investigate what's true and what's not true with no judgement. I can look forward to the opportunity to nurture my true Self that has been there all along. My ego dissolves as it's my true Self that I'm protecting. Practicing acceptance, surrender, and trusting the process all help me focus on what I can do for myself. This gives me courage and strength to take the next step to move forward. It's remembering one day at a time, one step at a time, and one activity/task at a time. I can give myself a break when things get messy.

A meditation practice can be a pausing moment when facing distrust. The other day I felt in my heart and chest an overwhelming sense of how distrust and blaming another can bring intense pain. My understanding about the eight-fold path allowed me to respond differently. The mantra I repeated to myself was, "look forward to emotional abandonment and look towards yourself." I smiled. I was reminded that my higher power is giving me the chance to reconnect with myself and do the things that provide safety, peace, compassion, love, and expansion in my heart. I don't have to continue to defend myself with negativity. I can practice my self-care tools and move my energy in a loving, self-compassionate way. This is everlasting healing and my brain has a chance to rewire to responses that serve me more and more.

Reflection Questions:
What does distrust mean to you?

Have you been hurt before from distrust in others and/or yourself?

Have you ever been accused of being distrustful?

With self-compassion, what have you learned about yourself from distrust?

Have you ever given trust to someone when you sensed, in your gut, a feeling of distrust? If yes, was your intuition true?

What prevented you from following your gut intuition?

What are some of your biggest fears as it relates to trust in others? Or self? Or in the process?

What are some mindful meditation/yoga practices to help you develop a personal pause when facing distrust?

How would it feel to self-nurture verses fight and argue after experiencing distrust?

Who/what can you include in your network of support when facing distrust? (This is a reminder to know we are not alone. It's courageous to do the self-care that brings resilience, growth, and freedom of the mind.)

#27

FALSE SENSE OF CONNECTION

Identity cannot be found or fabricated but emerges
from within when one has the courage to let go.
~Doug Cooper

A false sense of connection can be rooted from a fear and ego-based lifestyle. It can lead to short-term happiness yet leave us feeling emptier and as if we have a hole in our heart.

Fear can arise from feelings of abandonment and that we may be left alone. We can resist the truth. Anger and resentment can be the driving force to argue and feel as if we are right. Negativity feeds more negativity on the merry-go-round. There will be extreme ups and downs to deny and protect the insanity of unhealthy boundaries. Sometimes it feels like, 'Game on' and the goal is who wins and who is right. It's an imbalance of energy.

The Universe mirrors to me my rooted feeling from my fears. If I fear being abandoned, I recreate patterns in my life that expose me to more abandonment. I can live awake or asleep. I can react or respond to my higher consciousness. The only way to heal is to connect from within, look towards myself to nurture, and connect with something greater than myself to ground and recover. There is no one that can heal that feeling inside if I don't find my own personal healing practice to honor my grief.

> In the middle of difficulty lies opportunity.
> ~Albert Einstein

It's been through many moments of painful relationships that I awakened the movement of my own self-care. It was through my own addiction that I built a passion to learn more about recovery and healing my body holistically.

> Saying no can be the ultimate self-care.
> ~Claudia Black

I say 'no' more to power struggles. I don't try to defend myself in an argument like I used to and try to have the last word. Instead, I save my energy and keep my words more peaceful. I say 'no' to engaging with those who want to argue. I smile and go inward. I say 'no' to pretending that things in my life should be perfect. I say 'no' to feeling the urge to go to the corners and crevices of a conversation of what is right and wrong, what is good and bad, and what I/they should and shouldn't do. I say 'no' to what doesn't serve me and bring me ultimate compassion.

Pride blocks my heart. To heal from suffering, my true Self comes from that space in my heart that vibrates compassion. It is my ego and my fears that can feed my false sense of connection. It is through my experience that I know that pattern/habit no longer serves me. As we say in yoga, 'let go of what doesn't serve.' Our practice can honor and serve us in a more long-term therapeutic way to sustain recovery.

The Power of Thought by Mahatma Gandhi says your beliefs, thoughts, words, actions, habits, and values all connect with your destiny. With this in mind, no pun intended, my thoughts can serve me or destroy me. Each day I can be grateful to wake up and start a new day, a new beginning and practice mindfulness. I chose to live rather than die. I am not getting younger and know that I have less energy to fall into my own mental traps. I want to practice more compassion to awaken my consciousness.

Reflection Questions:
In what ways have you grieved losses in relationships?

In what ways have you connected with relationships that are temporary bandages over rooted fear and/or pain?

In what ways have you neglected your self-care to maintain a false sense of connection to others?

When knowing you are partaking in a false sense of connection, what does this numb temporarily? (For example Facebook/internet/television can allow me to feel 'sort of' connected and numb out to boredom or restlessness)

What have you learned about yourself when it comes to a false sense of connection with others and/or self?

How can the power of the pause help you nurture the hole in your heart to recover and take better care of your true self?

How does self-compassion diffuse an argument with another?

What are some healthy habits you can do when you look towards yourself verses numbing in the midst of feeling separation from self and/or others?

#28

IDENTITY CRISIS - THIS IS NOT ME...OR IS IT?

Everything changes when you start to emit your own frequency rather than absorbing the frequencies around you, when you start imprinting your intent on the Universe rather than receiving an imprint from existence.

~Unknown

There is the ego and the true Self. An identity crisis can be an internal conflict that involves the ego and the true Self. The ego is how I identify myself through what I do, what I have, my physical attributes, my power over others, my pride, my individual identity and a sense of distinction/separation from others, etc. My true Self is more about my internal richness that involves self-reflection, honesty, humility, self-compassion, compassion for others, connection with something greater than myself, and a sense of universal connectedness.

There is a distinction between the ego and the true Self. With greater awareness, I can know the difference. I can identify myself more with my true Self for long-term happiness and recovery. I can balance out my ego and observe my tendencies and patterns from how my ego has served me and gotten me off course. I can recognize when my ego/pride kicks in and how can I balance that out with my true Self, so I can come from a place in my heart.

My ego has helped and hindered me. Some ways that my ego has helped me has been through facing some challenges, taking pride in my strengths, independence, and my victories. On the other hand, I have observed that my ego has built up my pride in ways to fight for my beliefs aggressively, hurt others through my words and actions, blame and shame others to feel better, keep buying and working to make more and more money for my sense of worthiness, and so forth and so on. Looking back, when I stay in my ego mind I can drift further away from my true Self.

> The measure of intelligence is the ability to change.
> ~Albert Einstein

Facing my ego with self-compassion and allowing my true Self to grow and heal is important to allow energetic shifts. This process helps me connect more with myself and my higher power. This awakening can feel quite overwhelming with emotions of losses/grief. It's okay to allow, recognize, investigate and nurture yourself. It is a beautiful unique process for each one of us.

Like ongoing recovery, awareness of the ego and true Self is a day to day check in. It takes mindful practice to observe patterns from ego with self-compassion. When looking at our ego, the other door can lead us to our underlying fears, weaknesses, and past stories that aren't serving. These are opportunities to reconnect and get to know oneself more than ever. Be patient. It's a process.

Reflection Questions:
What are some of your ego characteristics? (For example, controlling, productive, etc)

How have they served you? (Gaining financial freedom, more confidence)

How have they been destructive? (For example, my confusion as my self-worth is not the value of my productivity)

What are some of your true self characteristics/nature? (For example, creative being, compassionate, childlike, passionate, natural, etc.)

Have you ever forgotten your true Self from being more in your ego self?

What grief/losses have you experienced from forgetting your true Self? (For example, loss of time from staying busy, speaking out of anger and hurting another for revenge, not enjoying life more due to stressors, less time spent in creativity, loss of sense of true Self. etc.)

What opportunities and gifts can come from awakening your true Self? (For example, peace, less fear, sense of worthiness, etc)

In what ways have you grown and changed from looking back? (For example, being a better friend to myself, having your own back no matter what, acceptance, surrendering, etc)

What are some things you can do to help strengthen your mind to be present with your true nature and aware when your ego is activated? (For example, self-compassion, reflection, pausing, meditating, taking a walk, pause when your pride is hurt, speak from the heart, looking towards yourself for love and safety)

#29

HEALING LOVE ADDICTION

Help each other grow instead of destroying each other.
~Buddhist quote

Addiction can come in different forms other than alcohol and drugs. A common addiction is love addiction. This addiction involves relationships that have unclear boundaries, inappropriate behaviors, a gut/intuitive feeling that can bring unsettling feelings, and a pattern of pain/suffering experiences occur.

Often, these love addiction relationships stem from underlying conditions from childhood. Emotional abandonment, an absent parent, emotional/physical trauma can all be examples of untreated energy trapped in the body.

Untreated, these patterns of behavior in relationships can progress and repeat. Choices can lead to high risk behaviors that lead to drama, unhealthy boundaries, and a vicious cycle of pain and distrust. Through conscious awareness, mental health counseling, and support (Al-Anon®, 12 Step Programs, yoga), self-compassion, there are ways to recover and modify neurological imprints in the brain.

In yoga, mindfulness helps connect the body, mind and spirit. My mat is a space to come back to, take a pause, connecting to my breath, being still and/or moving my breath through my system. As I continue to come back to my mat and my own practice, I start to build a tool for long-term recovery. I can apply this repetition mentally, physically, and spiritually in other areas of my life, like love addiction.

As I'm more aware of my own patterns that don't serve me in a relationship, I can reprogram my brain through mindful practice. This is a process. Instead of being in fear, reacting, and ultimately escalating my energy negatively, I can go inward with compassion. I can recognize where the discomfort is in my body (like my chest/heart/throat) and recognize the story I say to myself. This is a wonderful opportunity to look towards myself.

> Being in recovery does not mean immunity of pain;
> it means learning to take loving care of ourselves
> when we are in pain.
> ~Melody Beattie

I give to myself the self-compassion verses abandoning myself. I can show up for myself in a way that no one else can. How can I love another if I'm not loving my true Self? I'm learning to love me unconditionally more and more.

Some new habits/patterns I go to when I feel the discomfort are self nurturing activities. These choices show me that I honor, love, and respect myself. I eat a warm healthy meal. I write/journal. I talk to a friend. I rest. I walk. I take an Epsom salt bath with my favorite essential oil. I do yoga/ meditation. I light a candle, or I perform a sacred ritual like burning sage or Palo Santo. I massage my feet and hands with oil. I say mantras to myself like "look forward to emotional abandonment and look towards self!" I am recreating rituals/habits that are serving me and bringing me back to the present. My mind has a tendency to go to the story stuck in the past and fearing the future. This no longer serves me.

> As I take a deep cleansing breath, I'm present with all of this and I let it go with a longer exhale!

I'm surrendering in a way that embraces fear and faces it with self-inquiry. No judgement as this is process. It doesn't have to be perfect. It can be messy. The key is to give to myself from a loving place. I remind myself that 'I'm here and I love me.' I remind myself that "I have your back and your heart right now." That's totally different from my responses before as I would go down a dark rabbit hole. The pain and suffering were unbearable. I would get angry and want to get even through my language and/or actions. I would feel my heart race and I would cry. In the past, I attached my self-worth to exterior circumstances. "I must not be good enough. Why is this happening? This isn't fair. I'm in pain." During this time, I would identify myself with what was happening. That has nothing to do with who I am. I am a loving, kind-hearted, beautiful person who is whole and healing.

Nurturing myself is not selfish. It's a passage to my internal medicine. This is an experience of creating that space and place in my heart that allows me to heal my underlying conditions. It's a process that holds me accountable to watch my back and protect it with safety and compassion. I don't judge myself. I protect myself not just through my actions but also through my own speech. Like yoga, it is my own practice. I keep coming back and arriving to my heart. I pause and move the energy in a healthy way.

My home in my heart is a place that I can take time to take care of myself and be present. My active recovery allows me to face love addiction with greater awareness to my patterns, choices, inner fears, and a ton of forgiveness. I put the focus back on me rather than the other person. I surrender trying to fix, control, convince, argue, or chase others to get love. I remove myself from the victim state and make choices that protect me. There is no wrong or right. It isn't a comparison. It's a place of compassion, safety, and awareness. It's not only one day at a time, it's one cleansing breath at a time.

Building tools to work with and doing my self-care is important. It's a part of ongoing recovery. There will be days that I forget what I know. If I'm tired, impaired, sad, etc., I can become vulnerable. I can make choices not thinking clearly. This can be a sabotaging behavior. Exercise caution when you have a history of love addiction or any compulsions. Some people abstain from impairing substances, avoid impairment, toxic people and toxic environments to lower their risk factors. Remember it's your practice so you get to develop a long-term plan that serves you!

In Sanskrit, "svadhyaya" means self-study. It is part of the eight-fold path in Buddhism. When facing my patterns/habits that don't serve me with a compassionate heart, I can shift my energy into habits/patterns that protect my values. I can look towards myself and start from within the mind. This takes practice and patience.

Developing techniques to investigate the areas in my life that I feel stuck or want to change personally are helpful. "Is the story I tell myself true?" as Byron Katie asks in her book *The Work*. Her method helps me do lots of self-inquiry to hear what my mind says to myself. It allows me to hear what I tell myself, how this makes me feel, my attachments to my story, my fears, and I can rewrite my story to obtain more peace, love and freedom. It allows me to get unstuck energetically in my mind through my story. I am tapping into my true Self and moving the energy that feels binding. I bring more truth and work on my personal story that helps my mind be set free. I surrender to the sense of trying to control others.

Then, I can allow my body to pause and feel what it is that I need. It's an inward investigation and self-inquiry with no judgement. Am I being prideful? Am I connecting with the love in my heart? Which one? I have been told that if I come from a prideful place, I literally block my heart and my true Self. 'My ego isn't my amigo!' I remind myself I just want peace and serenity.

> When you find no solution to a problem, it's probably not a problem to be solved, but rather a truth to be accepted.
> ~Buddhist quote

Reflection Questions:
When doing some self-study, what are some truths that are difficult to accept? (For example, with self-compassion and nonjudgement, I am aware that I am sometimes too friendly with the opposite sex and can open up unclear boundaries that don't serve me. This can send out unclear messages that I can be more aware and mindful to prevent unhealthy patterns.)

How would you describe a toxic relationship? A love addiction? (For example, verbal abuse, low self-esteem, painful when loving another)

Have you experienced a form of love addiction? If yes, how so?

What patterns do you experience? (For example, temper tantrums, power struggles, revenge, blaming, shaming, etc)

What were some of your greatest fears when facing chaos in these types of relationships? (For example, emotional abandonment, not trusting, feeling defeated, being taken advantage of or used, etc)

Do you have any trauma/PTSD/childhood losses that remind you of similar feelings when you experience pain/suffering from an addiction in a relationship? If so, how so? What are the feelings?

How did you react when feeling the pain/suffering from a love addiction?

What do you tell yourself when experiencing an unhealthy relationship? Do you hear any patterns in your story?

If you look forward to your greatest fear (ex. emotional abandonment), how can you look towards yourself for recovery? What can you do for yourself to help?

Who is a part of your support system besides yourself? (family, friend, 12 step programs, etc)

How can you pause, breathe, connect with your body, nurture yourself and then respond?

What are some activities that nurture your soul?

What do you want most in a love relationship?

How can self-compassion help you recover?

How can "pausing" when you sense an unhealthy pattern allow you to be more conscious in your mind?

Have you detoxed before?...not just for health reasons but also for the mind? How can a cleanse/detox benefit the healing process? (Ex: liver detox, purging alcohol, caffeine, sugar, or processed foods)

#30

REVENGE/HATE AND ITS KARMA

Weak people revenge. Strong people forgive.
Intelligent people ignore.
~Buddhist quote

Revenge is seeking out a "one up" on another after being hurt. It is seeking pain/suffering in another to get even. It's a controlling behavior that can feed an addiction.

> *How people treat you is their karma.*
> *How you respond is your karma.*
> *~Wayne Dyer*

Karma is an eastern philosophy that stresses the universal force that what I do and say can come back to me. It's a frequency that tunes me into my thoughts and sends a vibration that mirrors my energy back to me. Awakening your mind and being mindful of responding verses reacting helps align your true Self to the Universe.

> Don't waste your time on revenge. Those who hurt you will eventually face their own karma.
> ~Buddhist quote

Seeking revenge is like resisting what I'm powerless over and playing the role of my own higher power. When I am in my ego mind, my pride is wounded. I get angry, upset, and want to retaliate to get the other to feel pain. I want to give my wound a temporary bandage. This type of energy can be powerfully dangerous spiritually as it blocks my heart. My healing process can take longer and even be delayed. Often, I stay in my pain body more. I suffer more and amplify my problems. This behavior isn't sustainable. Eventually the energy can be draining, confusing and hopeless. It becomes harder to see clearly as I'm in the past and in the future. My ability to be present with my true Self takes the back seat. My ego becomes the driver! With this perspective, I see the darker sides of people and of myself.

Have you ever sought revenge on another and initially felt great and then later suffered? It's like a domino effect as I put more negativity out in the Universe, I get more negativity back from others or a "backfire" circumstance occurs to me. Some people call this a form of karma. I get back what I put out in the Universe.

Often times, it's common to lose our true Self, lower our self-esteem, be confused as to who my true Self is as I can attach my pain to my story and get stuck in my mind. I suffer. Others suffer. This drains creativity and the mind. It is not sustainable as the body can develop 'dis-ease.' Mental and physical health are drained if progressive.

Seeking revenge and hating another is the opposite of compassion. If I'm working on my alignment with my higher power and true Self through conscious connection, I will surrender my ego and pride. This is not weakness. Strength, courage and grace are developed and imprinted more in the mind and body. The benefits from surrendering to negativity and revenge are that my self-esteem boosts, healing energy enters my body, a sense of calmness arises, I have a greater awareness of the situation, and compassion for my true Self to do more of the things that lead to sustainable recovery.

This is a practice that is developed personally. It is there for me to arrive and come back to and pause. I am able to connect with my body, mind, and true spirit. I don't judge myself and others. I allow myself to feel and do the self-nurturing techniques after pausing and breathing. "I am here and present". I remind myself, "This shall pass" as I'm experiencing the discomfort. I practice self-control to get the outcomes that serve and honor me. "I smile" as a reminder of the Buddha nature.

The 'middle path' is another helpful recovery tool. This reminds me that nothing is perfect. My mind doesn't go to the judgements of what's right and wrong.

I am not the martyr to fix all problems in a way that I feel is best. I'm not righteous over the Universe. I surrender and trust the process as I am a spiritual being looking towards the light, not the dark. I accept others for who they are and allow them to experience their own experiences. I surrender control and the desire/need to change others even if I feel I'm right. I refrain from the games and bait of an argument. I speak my truth with compassion. I walk away and smile to the space, the place in my heart I call home. This is a practice for sustainable recovery.

> The best revenge for the people who hurt you is to show they are no longer the reason behind your smile and tears.
> ~Buddhist quote

Reflection Questions:
How does revenge make you feel short term?

How does revenge make you feel long term?

Do you believe in karma?

Are there any ways you can look back and sense a karmic experience? (Remember, it's important to stay with your self-compassion as this isn't about judgement)

How can you be more present and pause before reacting to a negative situation?

What can you do during 'the pause' to bring more self-compassion to your true Self?

What are the benefits from developing a practice to come back to when chaos, discomfort, and negativity arise?

Who/what can support you in developing a positive plan to sustain your active recovery?

How can you detach more from yourself when coming from a prideful place?

What are some mantras that can help you focus on your intentions?

~CLOSING~

REDEMPTION

The meaning of redemption is redeeming oneself, liberation, to be set free, an operation that saved oneself, and/or for usefulness or continued existence.

There are times in our life that we feel things are going well and there are times in our life that it feels just painful, low, and even unfair. Embracing both sides with compassion for self and others is a way of moving closer to the 'middle path' in Buddhism.

> *How do I honor the happy times and how do I equally honor the painful times?*

In my mind, how do I set myself free from my pain that binds my mind, body and spirit? This is a recovering moment. Life has glorious moments, pain and suffering, ups and downs, the losses and gains, pretty much all of it. Life can feel unfair. The Universe doesn't owe us anything. Life doesn't owe me anything. What I do with the low moments in my life is important for optimal healing to happen. It's all a process. Finding meaning in the low, hard times and moving that energy into a passion, or freedom, and strength is powerful. This is resilience and growth at its core. This is where we can tap into our own creative superpowers!

I'm a big fan of Frank Sinatra and I love the lyrics of Frank Sinatra's song, *That's Life*. I admire his music and know that like anyone, he had a ton of ups and downs and it shined through in his music. I think of his days with the *Rat Pack* and moments with Sammy Davis, Jr. They all experienced the good times and the moments in life that were the most challenging. It was through their creativity, passion, and love for music that brought their own redemption. In my opinion, this is what makes a legend and inspiration to use what you got and turn it into gold.

Looking back at the past, many challenges, and obstacles I have faced have turned into some of the greatest gifts presently. It didn't happen overnight. It wasn't a piece of cake to open my heart, eyes, and mind to the other doors either. Yes, there were moments I cried, felt like I was alone, things were ending, life was hard, and I feared the worst. Through patience, counseling, mentorship, family, support from empathetic people, I would say I could step forward even if I stepped back. I wanted change. I was tired of the same old outcomes. I wanted to live and have a higher quality of living mentally, spiritually, and physically. I have seen untreated addictions progress into moments of "death, institutions, and/or jail."

I knew I wanted to walk through the other door and wanted to shift my focus from what happened into how it would feel to find meaning, purpose, and freedom from my pain and suffering. With an open heart full of self-compassion, mentorship, and support, I awakened my true Self.

While getting my clinical supervision, my mentor told me that all experiences bring moments of learning and lessons. I had felt challenged by my previous experiences, and now I'm open to the gifts that came from those experiences. It happened already so what do I want to do with my story to continue to progress and recover?

If it wasn't for my childhood experiences, I wouldn't have gone on to use my bilingual skills to help teach English as a second language, work in the emergency room as a bilingual medical case manager, or become a clinician in mental health. I would not have had these particular callings/passions/gifts. It was through the grief that I found honor for others and myself more and more. It was being in the moment and accepting it all that gave me the courage to put one foot in front of the other with less shame or guilt.

There can be redemption with creativity, an open mind and an open heart. It's not easy work. It's not a job someone can do for me. I have to decide what it is that I want in my life and ask for help when I'm struggling. It's humility at its most beautiful level. Who would of thought that recovery can be a movement into finding our true Self? The old stigmas of addiction for me like: weak willed, ignorant, feeling sorry verses empathy are losing their power. My ego is no longer the front seat driver and my true Self in the back seat for the crazy ride.

Reflection Questions:
What are some times in your life that you have converted or can convert into redemption?

How does that make you feel when you have redeemed yourself from your past problems?

What brings you joy? What are some of your dreams?

When you look at yourself in the mirror, what do you say?

How can you become more compassionate with yourself to nourish your inner beauty?

What are some tools included in your personal recovery plan for optimal healing? What times in your week do you schedule time for self-care and reflection? (For example, Tuesday at 11am Al-Anon®, Thursday at 6pm yoga, daily mindful walks, etc.)

THE POWER OF THE PAUSE QUICK GUIDE

*What to do for yourself when faced with a
"now what?!" moment/situation.*

Ideas: walking, tea, pause, breathe, go outside and
get fresh air, meditate, hydrate, nutrition, rest, mantras
and yoga, call trusted friend, go to a meeting, read,
have a creative date with yourself, visualize your
AM/PM rituals to work on consistently, get a massage,
go to the beach, give yourself an electronic break, take a
day to rest, recharge and recover!

Add your own ideas below:

_____

_____

_____

_____

_____

_____

~NAMASTE~
MOVING FORWARD WITH
GRATITUDE

What an honor it has been to witness people recover and build support. What an honor it is to find meaning in addiction and my own recovery from the losses of a parent's and family's own personal addiction. Instead of separating from what happened, I find connection to something greater than myself. It becomes a spiritual journey through trusting and believing that there is a bigger picture, even if I don't see it.

It's doing one day/thing at a time. It's not doing it all at once and getting it all overnight or right. This is my life practice/cycle to make my recovery have life, breath, pausing moments, chaotic times to invite and sit with while having a cup of tea, it's honoring my grief and myself with the purest dose of self-compassion. It's showing up to my yoga mat and honoring the choice to make time for myself to pause, reset and recharge. It's allowing myself to give myself what I need and not put it off any longer. It's not judging myself for my mistakes and having more compassion for others I don't agree with (that can be a hard one depending on the situation). It can be a distraction without a mindful lens.

My physical and mental scars may be healed or still healing from the trauma, but I respect my experiences and turn over a lot of what I don't have control over to my higher power, nature, and/or something greater than myself. I surrender with love towards myself. I look in the mirror and remind myself how beautiful I am, how strong I am, how smart I am, and how I empathize with others for their journey. I forget sometimes. I do it all over again. There is no separation from my true Self. The ego loses power over the abundant beauty of my true Self.

I learned that it's my journey. My own uniqueness is what makes me special, including the messy parts. It's the showing up and coming back to my journey that allows me to heal, grow and make sense of it all. Not only am I developing more resiliency techniques, but I am also developing post traumatic growth. The 'middle path' reminds me to be open to all the *stuff* with less judgement and more compassion. Tonglen reminds me that through connection I can heal, love and always be present with something greater than myself. I'm never alone.

This journey is about finding your authentic self and your own authentic joy. It's finding your self-worthiness and value. It's coming home to that place inside you that welcomes you with love and compassion. It's coming back to your mat, showing up for yourself, pausing and breathing, laughing, finding joy, loving yourself, resting, and developing healthy boundaries. These experiences become even more inviting when you say, "I want to stay here and have more time to do this. This makes me calmer. I feel healthier. I'm more myself. I rest better. I'm happier in life. I'm not giving this up because I'm feeling alive!"

My hope for those suffering, struggling or stuck in the pain body is to "offer chaos a cup of tea" and lean into the discomfort and practice self-inquiry and nurturing to ground your true Self. I'm hoping that my stories of how I found honor in my grief will inspire others to do the same...to move forward and get unstuck with the energies and stories that no longer serve. I hope for liberation and redemption of the soul and spirit.

> *May all beings be happy, content and fulfilled. May all beings be healed and whole. May all beings have whatever they want and need. May all beings be protected from harm and free from fear. May all beings be awakened, liberated and free. May there be peace on earth and the entire universe.*
> *~Buddhist meta prayer*

REFERENCES & RESOURCES

1. Tara Brach R.A.I.N meditation, *Radical Acceptance* book
2. Nikki Myers Y12SR yoga teacher training, "the issues live in your tissues" - https://y12sr.com/about/nikki/
3. Eckart Tolke *Power of NOW* book – 'pain body' concept
4. Frances Murcherson -*Heal your Whole Body* book, "look forward to emotional abandonment and look towards yourself"
5. Pema Chodron - *When Things Fall Apart* book, "offer chaos a cup of tea"
6. Byron Katie - *The Work* book
7. Melody Beattie – *The Language of Letting Go* book
8. Brene' Brown – *Daring Greatly* book
9. Julia Cameron - *The Artist's Way* book – 'weekly art date and morning pages/journaling'
10. Healing Trauma/PTSD – *The Body Keeps the Score* book *by* Dr. Bessell Van der Kolk
11. Eight fold path - https://www.britannica.com/topic/Eightfold-Path
12. The Middle Path/Way - https://encyclopediaofbuddhism.org/wiki/Middle_Way
13. Thich Nhat Hahn - *Being Peace* book
14. Tonglen practice - https://encyclopediaofbuddhism.org/wiki/Tonglen
15. 12 Step Programs - https://www.samhsa.gov/find-help/national-helpline

ABOUT THE AUTHOR

Frances Angeline Rowe has a master's degree in Mental Health Counseling and is a Licensed Clinical Addictions Specialist and Certified Clinical Supervisor. She has been working in the addictions counseling field for 20 years and has been in private practice for 16 years. She is also a Y12SR Yoga instructor, artist, meditator and beach lover.

You can contact her at:
Website: https://dwiservicesnc.com/
Email: dwiservices@bellsouth.net

ABOUT THE PUBLISHER

Positive Energy Publications

More titles by Positive Energy Publications:

How to Organize with Ease: Easy to Follow Steps for Garages, Closets, Junk Drawers and More...

7 Simple Steps to Non-Toxic Gardening: A Guide for the Overwhelmed, Eco-Conscious, First-Time Gardener

Rivers of Change Channels of Hope: A Mental Health Survivor's Guide Through Lived Experience

Finding your Soulmate after 40: The Smart Woman's Guide

Navigating Career Changes after 40: The Soulful Woman's Guide

30 Days to Happier Ways: The Journal

Positive Energy Oracle Cards: Companion Guide

Unleash your Intuitive Superpowers

#BrokenHearted Wisdom

#WholeHearted Wisdom

#WholeHearted Wisdom – Poetic Journal

3,2,1 No More Pain

Made in the USA
Columbia, SC
12 June 2020